SIMON HASLAM

CONSULTING SKILLS FOR SOCIAL RESEARCHERS

POLICY PRESS SHORTS POLICY & PRACTICE

First published in Great Britain in 2017 by

Policy Press
University of Bristol
1-9 Old Park Hill
Bristol
BS2 8BB
UK
+44 (0)117 954 5940
pp-info@bristol.ac.uk
www.policypress.co.uk

North America office:
Policy Press
c/o The University of Chicago Press
1427 East 60th Street
Chicago, IL 60637, USA
t: +1 773 702 7700
f: +1 773 702 9756
sales@press.uchicago.edu
www.press.uchicago.edu

© Policy Press 2017

British Library Cataloguing in Publication Data
A catalogue record for this book is available from the British Library.

Library of Congress Cataloging-in-Publication Data
A catalog record for this book has been requested.

ISBN 978-1-4473-3386-9 (paperback)
ISBN 978-1-4473-3388-3 (ePub)
ISBN 978-1-4473-3389-0 (Mobi)
ISBN 978-1-4473-3387-6 (ePdf)

Cover design by Policy Press
Front cover: image kindly supplied by iStock
Printed and bound in Great Britain by CMP, Poole
Policy Press uses environmentally responsible print partners

Contents

Acknowledgements

In appreciation of the Social Research Association's work in promoting high quality social research. And acknowledging the work of the Institute of Consulting and the International Council of Management Consulting Institutes, in professionalising consulting practice. Thanks also to colleagues at FMR Research Ltd for the practical insight into consulting skills in social research projects over the past two decades.

List of figures

1
CONSULTING AND SOCIAL RESEARCH

The purpose of *Consulting skills for social researchers* is to offer insight from the world of consulting to social researchers. As knowledge workers, social researchers and consultants share much in common in terms of the application of their experience and skills. Social researchers and consultants work with data, in its creation and its analysis. Social researchers and consultants are engaged in projects – specific areas of work each with a start and finish – often more than one at a time, and both social researchers and consultants aim to make a positive contribution to their clients (whether these clients are internal or external ones).

Despite these similarities, there are differences. This book seeks to draw on the practice of consultants and offer this knowledge to those working in social research, as a means of potentially bringing added dimensions to their portfolio of understanding and skills.

1 Social research and consulting – key distinctions

While the intention is not to turn social researchers into consultants, the distinctions between social research and consulting provide a platform for social researchers to reflect on their own areas of work.

Social researchers and consultants share an interest in solving problems, but the emphasis of each discipline is different. Social research places emphasis on the understanding, the development of insight or the creation of a conceptual understanding of what is being observed or presented. The focus is the codification or theoretical interpretation – the result of a capably applied programme of systematic investigation – which creates intellectual property, and potentially learning to be shared. A consultant is more likely to focus on practice, that is, the application of the theory or conceptual understanding; moving the fruits of research on to their application.

Social research usually places a high emphasis on process and provenance around data (be it qualitative or quantitative) as the foundation of understanding. The higher attention for consultants is typically devoted to 'clients', people affected by the application of research as the recommendations arising from studies are translated into actions. Usually the consultant draws heavily on their personal knowledge or experience as it applies to a client situation, which often leads to the creation of intellectual property which is unique to a specific context. As such, much consulting is to do with change and the implications of things being done differently to the way they have been done to date.

It is on this pathway around the conversion of research findings into implemented recommendations that the field of consulting probably has most to offer social research. With appropriate judgement and application, the tools and techniques of consulting can possibly extend the impact of well-conducted research.

My own firm, FMR Research, has for the last 17 years linked these two areas of work. We have applied consulting approaches to social research projects to help the translation of research findings into changes in the way services are provided, for example in health services provision and in local government. We have also underpinned organisational consulting projects by robust social research to valuable effect, on one occasion being nominated to represent the UK at the international management consulting awards for the operational review of a prominent child-care organisation.

Around social research, the term 'consulting' is open to multiple interpretations, and it is used in different ways. This includes consulting and research firms contracting with client organisations, research teams within larger organisations who are working with 'internal' customers, and researchers looking to enhance the influence of their work on policy and administration. None of the interpretations is necessarily incorrect, although the differences between them can muddy the waters somewhat. We are concerned with the overlap between the areas of social research and consulting and where this is potentially fruitful, across these varied domains.

2 The structure of this book

In many ways, Consulting Skills for Social Researchers is the book of the course. Since 2009, the UK's Social Research Association (SRA)[1] has, as part of its professional training programme, provided workshops under the same label. Myself and other team members have run open courses on Consulting Skills for Social Researchers in various parts of the UK and in-house workshops for larger organisations with an interest in this area (usually government or statutory bodies or larger research firms). The text is structured along the same lines as these workshops, the logic having been refined through application and reflection. The book has three main chapters which follow this introductory chapter:

- *Chapter 2* looks at *the ingredients* of consulting and goes further into how consultants apply theory and help move research results into practice.
- *Chapter 3* examines *the consulting process* and looks at the sequence of steps that underpin consulting projects from beginning to end. It picks out the main areas which social researchers have found beneficial in augmenting their own approaches.
- *Chapter 4* focuses on how consultants use *interpersonal skills* in order to be appropriately influential, challenging the client in order to strengthen the link between research and better practice

- The final chapter (*Chapter 5*) returns to the purpose of this book and *summarises the main messages* and threads by means of crystallising the potential contribution of consulting to the field of social research.

The insight into consulting practice comes from my own experience as a consultant over the past 25 years, the last 17 of which have been spent as co-owner and director of a social research and consulting firm, and the growing literature on the practice of consulting. Particular prominence has been given to the work of ICMCI Academic Fellows. The ICMCI (International Council of Management Consulting Institutes) is the body focused on the professionalisation of consulting across the world.[2] Its 'Academic Fellows' are people recognised as active in consulting thought leadership and the development of consulting practice. Incorporating insight from this source helps provide a strong foundation to the approaches being advocated.

Notes

[1] More information on the Social Research Association can be found on its website, www.the-sra.org.uk.

[2] For more information on the ICMCI, see www.cmc-global.org. The ICMCI owns the internationally recognised 'Certified Management Consultant' (CMC) qualification, which is a global standard of proficiency for individual management consultants.

2
KEY INGREDIENTS OF CONSULTING

This chapter seeks to outline consulting and begin to make the links with social research. It contains five sections:

- *Section 1* looks at the main components of consulting activity, drawing attention to underpinning concepts.
- *Section 2* explores how consulting can accomplish its main role, which is to be valuable to the client.
- *Section 3* introduces the three main paradigms that encompass consulting activity – they are all useful, and capable of being valuable to a client, but do so in different ways.
- *Section 4* emphasises the importance of trust-based relationships in consulting, and outlines the salient ingredients.
- *Section 5* looks at the role of ethics in practice (which will be familiar ground for many social researchers) and moves towards greater 'professionalisation' of consulting activity.

1 Components of consulting

1.1 Defining consulting?

There are many explanations of the term 'consulting' which seek to explain what consulting is about. They typically share four ingredients:

- *It's about independence*
  The first is about the consultant's independence from the context. This means standing outside of the organisation or group being consulted, with the dual characteristic of objectivity and detachment. It is from this detached position that most consulting work is able to add to the client's own perspective and help realise insight that might otherwise be unidentified. For someone external to the client organisation, the concept of independence is straightforward. It is less clear for those with 'internal' consulting roles or positions.

- *It's about 'advice'*
  The second factor is around advice, which is probably the common currency of all consulting work. Consulting is viewed as something in which a client's knowledge and/or capability is enhanced though the provision of advice. As we shall see, the term 'advice' requires a liberal interpretation, as there are several ways that advice can be both sourced and presented. Some advice is provided directly by the consultant based on his or her expertise, while other advice might arise from the consultant's facilitation of the client's view of the prevailing data, or indeed the client's own opinion.

- *It's about projects*
  Consultants talk about 'interventions', implying that consultants are temporary stakeholders in any client situation. An intervention will have a start point and also a finish – consulting is not a continual activity. In this respect, consulting work can be viewed as a project; a commercial consulting firm is typically an aggregation of various client project activities. The fact that the consultant tends not to be a permanent fixture within the client enterprise, and has a transitory presence, can help the consultant to have the objectivity that detachment brings.

- *It's about being valuable*
  The fourth ingredient is value. It is hoped that the result of consulting activity is seen as greater in worth to the client than the resources the client committed to it. The client exposes his

or her organisation to risk (reputational and operational) when opening themselves to consulting scrutiny, but the concept of value goes further than risk mitigation. Consulting should create a net gain for the client around whatever the client and consultant agree the focus of the work to be. The client may or may not spend money on the consulting activity, but the client will always need to invest time in a consulting project, which means the client incurs an opportunity cost whenever they use a consultant. Without a net gain consulting becomes parasitical, with the consultant feeding off the client, rather than beneficial. We look further into this point in Section 2, below.

1.2 Consulting involves many stakeholders

We made the point in the introduction that consulting is usually more concerned with the application of theory than its generation, which means much of consulting involves dealing with people as the conduits to putting ideas into practice. Consulting involves many stakeholder types, and 'stakeholder mapping' is the term used to describe the notion of understanding the array of the different groups of people who might be instrumental in or affected by the possible change. For example, a consultancy project, which involved exploring the feasibility of whether a bmx stunt track could be built into the middle of a cycle velodrome, needed to embrace the perspectives of the owners of the velodrome, the residents of the area in which the velodrome was located, the track cyclists who trained and raced at the velodrome, the bmx riders who sought their own cycling venue, other niche cycling communities who felt a legitimate claim to this space within the velodrome, and the part of the local authority responsible for promoting participation in sport and exercise across the local population. They did not all speak with one voice.

When mapping the landscape of stakeholders, the dimensions considered include the degree to which a stakeholder is able to wield power (some stakeholders are more powerful than others), the degree to which a stakeholder is interested in the issue or not (people who are engaged with an idea usually behave differently to those for whom it has low priority) the disposition of the stakeholder towards the idea (for example, supportive, ambivalent or potentially obstructive)[1]. In the translation of research findings into practice, consultants realise that stakeholder 'buy-in' (the acceptance of the idea) is key, and stakeholder mapping enables the recognition that different people need to be approached in different ways.

The stakeholder map does not drive the outcome of a consulting project (it would be highly unsatisfactory to focus on the majority of stakeholders to the exclusion of others), but it does help to shape the way that a consulting project can be designed. As a consulting project progresses, the shape of the stakeholder map also alters. The initial map represents a point of departure, but effective consulting seeks a course to be steered over this shifting terrain. Part of the consultant's repertoire, therefore, is an understanding of the implications of change and how people might react to it as the terrain shifts. This includes the characteristic negative reaction to change, as people feel more fearful of what they might lose compared to what they might gain, and also display such emotions as denial, anger and withdrawal.[2] A consultant is likely to be mindful of early successes ('quick wins' or 'low-hanging fruit') as a means of building momentum in a project to help it reach a tipping point, and needs to appreciate the distinction between 'home-grown' ideas (where the client figures out what to do themselves) compared to suggestions 'parachuted in' from external sources.

To develop a stronger feel for the focus and scope of any consulting work, we consider two things: the 'client system' and the 'dimensions' of a consulting engagement.

1.3 Client system

The effectiveness of consulting work in complex settings, such as those that apply in many social research areas, tends to be significantly enhanced when the consultant is able to comprehend the landscape of the various stakeholders and answer the question, which builds on earlier work by Edgar Schein: 'who is the client?'.

The idea of a client system draws on the work of ICMCI Academic Fellow Professor Andrew Sturdy and colleagues.[3] The term 'client' is used liberally in the consulting world, though not always with clarity of understanding. The not-for-profit sector might engage in a 'consultation exercise' with a certain client group (for example the residents of a local community, the users of a leisure facility, or people with a specific physiological condition), without first considering what power they are attributing to this group and what expectations are kindled through the consulting process. In the vast majority of cases, the communities being consulted are not the only senior stakeholders.

The route though the maze is made more straightforward by thinking of 'client' as a collective noun, rather than a single type of stakeholder. Within a 'client system' there are different genres of client.

- *Primary client* – the main contact for the consultant in the project (the main relationship for project commissioning, updates, management and commercial aspects).
- *Ultimate client* – the person / enterprise at the top – often the person who initiated the need and/or is funding the work, and is likely to derive some benefit from the consulting work (in getting something accomplished that was deemed important).
- *Intermediate client* – a category of individuals through whom the consultant needs to work in order to deliver the project objectives. These might include people responsible for setting up meetings or providing information, and people who are interviewed or attend focus groups as part of a consulting project. Effective consulting is largely dependent on good relations between the consultant(s) and all intermediate clients.
- *Proscribed client* – a category of individuals whose lives might be changed as a result of the consulting work: the people who will be affected by the outputs of the consulting project. This is a potentially broad category, so it is useful to look at it as degrees of change and to focus on the proscribed clients who are most strongly affected. Working with proscribed clients is pretty much

centred on the understanding of change psychology and the management of expectations.

These four are not hard-and-fast categories but help to provide a common language around the stakeholder map. In the field of social research, it is possible that a proscribed client might also be an intermediate client, for example, when a resident in a social housing scheme attends a discussion group organised by the consultant on the future of social housing in the area. A primary client might also be an ultimate client, for example when the chief executive of a policy think tank decides to commission a consulting project and assumes the role as the main contact with the consultant throughout the execution of the project.

1.4 The dimensions of a consulting engagement

Understanding the dimensions of a consulting engagement helps both consultant and client to share the expectations of how the consulting work might be valuable to the client, and defines the boundaries to the project. There are three dimensions of a consulting engagement, as described by Newton:[4]

Figure 2.1: The dimensions of consulting engagement

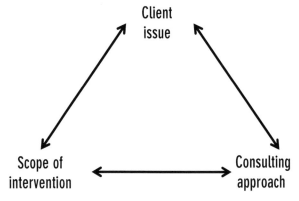

- *Client issue* – sits at the top of the triangle that links the three dimensions. The 'client issue' recognises that the driver for all consulting work should be a client with a need for something to be resolved. This can be referred to as the 'what'. In many situations a client will express this in an invitation to tender or a bid document. In some cases the 'what' will emerge from exploratory, pre-contract, discussions between the client and consultant, the result of which is greater clarification of thought on behalf of the client. And in other cases, the real 'what', that is, the real purpose of this consulting work, sits in the background as an unarticulated requirement. The two questions a consultant may wish to return to throughout a consulting project, and which help to focus their efforts are: 1) what value will my work bring to the resolving of the client's issue?; and 2) why is this work necessary?
- *Scope of intervention* – as we have said above, the term 'intervention' refers to the work the consultant will be doing when he or she intervenes in the client system. Consulting work has a start and a finish, and has a cost attached to it, together with expected deliverables. Consulting interventions are usually organised with the help of project management methods. Between the start and finish dates, there might be milestone dates or cut-off points.

The cost of consulting work can involve the payment of money as well as the investment of time. The consultant usually charges the client a fee for his or her expertise, but may decide to carry out some of the work pro bono. Usually, consultants charge for their time on a per diem basis, but sometimes it is on a results basis with remuneration commensurate with output (this is the dominant model in fields like recruitment consulting). Whereas the bulk of the cost of a consulting project is typically staff time, consulting work often carries additional direct costs for items like travel, venue hire, participation fees, and specialist sub-contracted input. For an internal consultant, the costs of the project are likely to be in the form of an agreed amount of time that the internal consultant will devote to the project, and perhaps an internal budget transfer from the client part of the organisation to cover these costs. A consulting intervention is highly likely to need the client's investment of time too, as a minimum to cover the client's work at commissioning meetings, project management and final sign-off. Bounded by the time and cost is the articulation of what the consulting project will deliver: the specification for the work. Project objectives should be sufficiently clear for both client and consultant to share the understanding of what the consulting project should accomplish.

- *Consulting approach* – this is how the consultant will organise the resources available within the available time and budget to deliver the consulting objectives. The nature and sequencing of the activities within the project is determined by the consulting approach, and vice versa. The consulting approach also encompasses the consulting style and the processes used by the consultants on the project. The point here is that the approach the consultant should take ought to be driven by the understanding of the issue the client faces (or thinks they face), and executable within the agreed scope of intervention. For example, in a review of the national approach to business mentoring, the issue the client (a national government) faced was one of tax revenue. Better-performing businesses generate higher tax income, directly and indirectly. Recognising that the project was about the protection and growth of non-subsidised jobs, plus the development of additional revenue, the consultancy focused on where the impact of mentoring would be most strongly felt, and the structure and processes by which mentoring could be most effectively and efficiently delivered across a country.

2 Adding value

2.1 How consulting can add value

Being valuable to the client should remain a core focus in any consulting activity. The complication is that what is considered as valuable consulting input can vary from project to project. Ideally, the client's expectations of what is valuable, how the consultant contributes value, and how that value is assessed after the event should align. Problems can arise when these are out of step.

The reasons why clients call upon the services of consultants vary. Although these categories are not necessarily independent of each other, each of them has implications for consultants looking to orient their input in a helpful way.

- *Access to skills* – in some cases the contribution that consultants make is providing access to skills the client does not possess. Often the fact that the client does not have these skills makes sound economic sense. The skills might have temporary utility, so it makes sense for the client to 'buy them by the yard' rather than incorporate them as a permanent fixture in their business. Skills that seem in particular demand in a social research context, and seem to function well within a consultancy model, include data analytics, data visualisation, project management, impact evaluation (including social return on investment), and stakeholder engagement. The skill of being able to independently facilitate a discussion falls into this category as well. Bringing an outsider in enables that person to manage the discussion process, allowing the client group to focus purely on content. For the most part, the contribution the consultant makes is a technical one.
- *Access to a specific methodology* – this is the next step along the pathway described above. On occasion, consulting enterprises can create distinct intellectual property which has commercial appeal; meaning clients like it and are prepared to pay money for it. There are examples of this where the consulting firms are accredited to provide the methodology (such as the Investors in People approach that became popular in the UK in the 1990s, and the more recent appetite for International Organization for Standardization (ISO) quality standards. The methodology in question uses the skills of the organisation, but it can also

be presented and protected in such a way that the consulting firm almost becomes the only game in town for any client organisation seeking to access the methodology. Gallup achieved this successfully with its Q12[5] employment engagement product, and the UK's Cabinet Office and consulting firm Capita jointly own the PRojects IN Controlled Environments (PRINCE2) project management methodology. For the originators of such a methodology there is substantial development investment which is committed without guarantee of return. If the recipe generates client appeal, the rewards are relative competitive immunity and a relatively standard recipe which can be re-sold to different clients.

- *Original idea* – in some instances, what consultants bring is a spark of creativity to the client. The consultant's position of detachment is probably a helpful vantage point from which to bring in different perspectives or provocative thinking as alternatives to the client's position, which usually centres on the here and now of a current operational model. This point has been illuminated by strategy consulting firm McKinsey and Company, who talk about the current business model of an enterprise being 'horizon one',[6] and step changes in approach design designated by subsequent horizon numbers. Characteristically, a client organisation finds it easier to have 'horizon one' discussions as that is the world it inhabits. When it comes to seeking pathways to different horizons, external input can be particularly helpful.

- *No free time* – this form of consulting help is referred to by some as 'bodyshopping'. In this situation the client knows what needs to be done and also how to do it, but lacks the capacity to execute. The value the consultant brings is in the form of extra 'arms and legs' to augment the client's core resource. Intellectual input isn't necessarily valued, neither is the consultant's own approach – moreover a departure from the client's own plan could be viewed as a shortcoming. And as the intellectual element of this type of consulting intervention rests pretty much with the client, remuneration for consultants is comparatively low, and commercial approaches under this model are often geared around volume and timescale. The margins are small, so consulting income is a very much a function of volume here.

- *Objective view* – sometimes the client seeks an independent assessment of the situation. The phrase 'can't see the wood for the trees' epitomises the challenges of being insightful when immersed in a situation. Sometimes the client has arrived at their own conclusion but needs the reassurance from a second pair of eyes before feeling confident enough to proceed. In some cases this form of consultancy can be beset by problems relating to the low perceived contribution from the consultants. Similar to criticisms about process consulting as an approach, there may well be occasions where the objective view from the consultants leads to a view that the client's own conclusions were indeed sound. Detractors might see the consultants as having contributed nothing: "We knew all this already"; but the converse should be closer to reality. This form of consulting delivers confidence to the client, equipping them with a greater strength of conviction as they enter the next phase of the work. So the response from the consultant to the client, when the client says something like: "You haven't told us anything we didn't already know", ought to be "Fantastic! If both of us have looked at the same data independently and come to the same view, you can be more confident that you're on the right track, which equips you well as you implement the idea".

- *To legitimise a decision* – extending on from the ability to provide an objective view, the consultant's value might come from the strength of their brand. Often, clients use consultants to independently endorse a proposition, the objective standpoint of the consultants together with their reputation in the particular area of work combining here to provide the 'ooomph' to raise the status of the work.

This is more than rubber-stamping – the brand value that the consultants offer can enable clients to achieve results which would be beyond them if they acted alone. In 2010, my firm lost a bid (we came second) to carry out a review of the first ten years of an organisation specialising in sexual health. The successful bidder was one of the well-known London-based consulting firms. Whereas I have little doubt that my team would have carried out the review with the same high (or even higher) level of competence as our competitor, our brand strength as a boutique social research and consulting firm based in Scotland was nothing like that of the one whom the client selected. The importance of this was readily inferred from the bidding documents for the work, which referred to the client organisation's dependence on external funding sources, a shifting landscape in the UK's focus on sexual health, and a keenness of this organisation to celebrate its achievements over its first ten years of work.

The above are not all the reasons why clients bring in consultants. Many external providers will be familiar with upturns in the interest in their services towards the end of their clients' financial cycles. When the funding model is rooted in the 'use it or lose it' paradigm, firms can win work by being available when clients need to use their budgets at the end of the financial year.

The challenge for the consultant is one of interpretation and understanding. It may be possible at the pre-project stage for the consultant to appreciate the particular angle on 'value' the client is looking for. If not then, it ought to be surfaced at the commissioning meeting when mutual expectations of client and consultant are aired. The way a consultant approaches a project if they are being employed in a 'bodyshop' context is very different to the way they would frame the work if the client was looking for an independent, objective view.

2.2 How consulting input can be evaluated

There are different ways in which the value of consulting input can be assessed, often driven by the issue the client is facing and the nature of the consulting intervention. The main point here is that while some consulting interventions can be evaluated on the basis of return on investment, some cannot and are best viewed through other evaluative lenses:

- *Return on investment* – the most obvious approach to evaluating consulting input is return on investment. Here, the monetary value of what the consulting work has realised is offered up against the client's investment in the consulting project. The return on investment approach to evaluation works most effectively if two conditions exist. The first is that the causal link between what the consultants do or recommend and the consequence is clear. The second is that the time-lag between the work and the results is short.

  Two regular candidates which merit evaluation through this lens are funding bids and operational improvements. In 2008, my firm was commissioned to carry out a consultation process to research and refine a service model to address unmet social need in a particular community. The second stage of the commission involved working with the client to build a business plan to provide a service that was attractive to external funders. The client's investment of under £30,000 in our services helped the client to secure external support in excess of £1,500,000 to bring the idea to reality. The scope for operational improvements in an organisation tends to be strongest when there is the option to use technology as a basis for service re-design, or when step changes in organisational structures (for example mergers) provide the opportunities for synergies to be explored with the consequential savings. In 2009/10, we provided such support to two neighbouring local authorities in the UK who saw the opportunity to enter into a shared services agreement with each other, as a vehicle to maintain service scale and quality in the face of budget pressures, by de-duplication where overlaps existed and by scale economies. Our bid was considered in relation to the realisable cost savings. There might also be the opportunity for consulting work of a developmental nature to be evaluated in this way. In these cases, consultants may explore the viability for the client to expand traded services, but this can be muted by the fact that the work is more speculative in nature. Some years ago, in Scotland, there was a case where a rural community pledged undying allegiance to the rail network should their local railway station be re-opened. In the event, the re-opened station remained underused, as the bulk of those consulted stayed in their cars. This form of consulting is also dependent on the client organisation having both the appetite and the capability to follow through with the recommendations to enhance their footprint, which is not always the case. In the private sector, evaluation of business development opportunities by transaction cost economics is easier than it is in other sectors. Some years ago I was part of a consulting team which helped a client (a packaging company) determine its best next steps in milk bottle packaging. Within two years, the costs of the tooling the client needed to commit to for the recommended new size of bottle were successfully recouped as sales grew.

Where impacts are less straightforward, the transaction cost economics approach is further complicated by how non-financial consequences are brought back to the common denominator of money. Considerations such as triple bottom-line reporting (profit, planet and people) and social return on investment are beginning to develop ways in which broader and more enlightened outputs might be accounted for.

- *Pollination* – this view of evaluation considers the merits of consulting activity relating to the role of consultants in the spreading of ideas. If organisations are flowers in the garden, consultants are the butterflies and bees. The fact that consultants see a lot, across a range of different organisations, places them strongly as a source of ideas around organisational practice. Without the input of consultants it can be difficult for a flower to learn about new stuff, especially in the detail that can be required to operationalise it.

The perspective for evaluation now becomes a comparison between the consultants and alternative sources of ideas / practice, and consideration of the consequences should the organisation choose not to make the investment. While this can appear as seeking to justify the role of consultants through a client's insecurity or fear, it does acknowledge the privileged position of consultants as observers of and commentators on sectors of business. Over the past 30 years, the management sector has seen the growth of consulting firms as thought leaders. Embeddedness theory talks to the client's ability to capitalise on the consultant's own intellectual capital.

There is a shadow side of organisational behaviour that flatters embeddedness theory, which is the characteristic of mimetic isomorphism.[7] Mimetic isomorphism describes when an organisation copies what other organisations in its sector do, primarily on the basis that if their peers are doing it, it is probably the right thing to do.

- *Legitimacy* – this third category brings together the objective perspective and the legitimacy that consultants can bring. It is about the use of consultants to enable an organisation to have something that otherwise it would not have had. The endorsement of an idea by the consulting team can raise the status of the idea and move it into fruition, with an ease which would have been hard to envisage without the consulting support. This can be for the entire organisation or, as is often the case in larger enterprises, for the direct benefit of one part of the organisation (for example, helping the leisure and communities team within a local authority champion its cause in the face of pressures from other service areas) as it seeks to muster overall support for an initiative. The activity that otherwise would not have happened becomes the result.

3 Types of consulting

Perhaps the most prominent landmark in the understanding of consulting skills was Ed Schein's illumination of consulting styles. Schein pointed out the distinction between three consulting approaches.[8] These are 'expert consultant', 'doctor-patient' and 'process consultant'. The three consulting approaches are quite different and each has merits and vulnerabilities:

- The *expert consultant* brings domain knowledge to the project. The expert's grasp of their subject equips them with the credentials and the capability to answer questions and give advice. We see expert consultants as members of consulting teams, bringing specific skills (for example fundraising) as part of larger programmes of work. Expert consulting has the potential to progress issues quickly. If the client is able to accept that the ownership of the solution rests with the expert, and values this expertise, then the pace of progress can be brisk. However, the underlying assumption is that the client is able to diagnose the problem to be addressed. For, just as expertise is deep, it is also narrow. The use of expert consultants presupposes that the client is accurate in their understanding of what expertise they need. We also see expert consultancy in the legal system where expert witnesses are brought into courts to give insight into specific subjects. Followers of crime fiction will be familiar with the idea of an 'expert witness' in legal proceedings. Here the expert consultant is a leading authority on the specific issue under question, for example, criminal behaviour or rail safety.
- The *doctor-patient* model is demonstrated in the way that many countries in the world approach medicine and the health of their populations. In the UK, the term general practitioner is used to describe the role of the local doctor. When a patient arrives at the doctor's surgery, the patient is likely to have already formed their own opinion of their condition. Many will have Googled their symptoms and arrived with a clear impression of what

they are suffering from. The skill of the general practitioner is their ability to listen to what they are being told, to probe and to draw on their breadth of expertise and bring their own judgement to the situation. Sufficient expertise enables them to look beyond the presented issue, and beyond just the symptoms. In many situations in this medical model, the patient is referred to expertise: consultants who are great specialists in a limited area, whereas in some situations the general practitioner has the capability to address the issue directly. Much consultancy in social research is based on this model. The generalist consultant has a good feel for the domain, and while the generalist lacks the depth of the expert, their breadth is a major attribute in situations which are riven with complexity, or where underlying issues have thus far escaped diagnosis.

- The process consultant is perhaps the opposite of the expert consultant. In process consulting the consultant seeks to harness the client's insight and facilitate what for a client is a journey of self-discovery. In his interview with Booz and Company's Traci Entel, Stephen Dubner likened the work of a process consultant to that of a therapist.[9] The main quality of good process consulting is that it gives the client ownership of the solution. The skill of the process consultant is not that they are the advice giver, but that they know how to choreograph the client's journey to enable the client to figure things out. It is based on the premise that the client is potentially the world's best authority on his or her situation. Process consulting is a 'how' skill as distinct from a 'what' skill. I met one consultant who had as his job title, on his business card, the title 'chaos pilot'. That told me all I needed to know about his approach. It is surely undisputed that clients owning solutions is a good thing, and that the act of creation is a powerful ingredient of ownership. Process consulting is not, however, without its drawbacks, as it presupposes that the client is capable of figuring out the solution. In the BBC series Mary Queen of Shops,[10] retail specialist Mary Portas (an expert consultant) brought transformations to the images of many of her clients, based on an insight into retailing of a depth that her clients were unlikely to have possessed. If this is the case, the technical quality of a solution arrived at by process consulting technique is limited. Another drawback is the time that can be consumed with process consulting. For the approach to add value, time has to be invested in the process. It requires involvement from the client side, together with a belief that the process is capable of delivering the results anticipated. Process consulting can suffer from the client post-project reflection that the client 'did all of the work', or that the client 'came up with the answers themselves' – the criticism that consultants steal your watch to tell you the time is widely shared.

In practice, a consulting intervention is likely to be a blend of all three of Schein's approaches. ICMCI Academic Fellow, Professor Tim Clark has spoken about the ideal consultant skills base being 'T' shaped, suggesting a sufficiently broad general capability melded with in-depth expertise in one area.[11] Professor David Megginson adds his view that domain expertise and process skills are not mutually exclusive. Expertise, he has said, gives you the ability to ask better questions.[12]

4 Trust

The reason why trust is so important in consulting is the risk that is inherent in change. Trust is about the willingness to be vulnerable to another party, and a willingness to take the risk. To go on trust implies being prepared to put yourself in the hands of others and expose yourself to that risk. There are some deep dives into the subject, and former Harvard Professor David Maister devoted an entire book to it.[13] One of the most practical ways of looking at trust is the trust equation.[14] This is based on four factors, three of which help build trust and one that is detrimental.

Figure 2.2: The trust equation

$$\text{Trust} = \frac{(\text{credibility} + \text{reliability} + \text{intimacy})}{\text{self orientation}}$$

- *Credibility* – the first potential trust builder is credibility. This is about how the credentials of the consultant are presented to and perceived by those being consulted. The starting point for many here is the CV or track record. At proposal stage, or even pre-proposal stage, the consultant's portrayal of their experience can help them to be favoured over competitors. The finesse necessary here relates to how information is presented. Norms of acceptability vary. In some contexts the appetite for credentials is high and the confident portrayal of a strong CV is *de rigueur*. In others, a more gentle approach, underselling, may be the most productive as it avoid the pitfalls of alienating the client or amplifying any insecurity the client might feel. In our firm's proposals, we don't include full CVs but half-page pen-pictures of each consultant on the team, customised to the project that is being bid for. Similarly, the firm's credentials for the job are kept sharp and focused, changing from proposal to proposal. Our logic is that we only include information that is appropriate to the potential project, and all the client reads about is relevant. We have competitors who take a different view and include full CVs for each consultant, presenting full experience profiles for their firms. Their logic is that, while this gives the potential client more to read, it also gives the client more power to decide what is relevant and what is not. Both approaches have merit and neither is perfect.

  The way that consultants are introduced has a bearing on the way they are viewed by other project stakeholders. The phrase 'bigging up' is descriptive of the process of one person helping build the perceived credentials of another. The role of social media and the internet also needs to be considered here. Consultants can reasonably expect their online profile to be scrutinised in parallel with anything they may submit to the client in the form of a proposal. So it behoves each consultant and each firm to be diligent here and ensure that, when they are Googled, what the search reveals is beneficial. Recently I gave some feedback to one particular consulting organisation about their website. Their landing page included the firm's news items, blog posts and twitter feed. The most recent news showing was two months old, the most recent tweet was over a year old, and the blog hadn't been added to for three years.

The major strength of credibility as a positive component of trust is that it is management. Consultants are not universally credible, just as trust is not a universal construct. But, with the right handling, credibility can be established strongly, almost from the word go.

- *Reliability* – the second trust factor is about whether the consultant is seen as reliable. In one respect, the translation of reliability to the consulting context is a straightforward one. It is about doing what you say you are going to do. The challenge is that one does not start with the reputation for being reliable. This is something that is earned and, if done well, grows in the course of a project. As it grows, so does the degree of trust. It is possible to accelerate the process by seeking opportunities to demonstrate reliability. I witnessed one of my colleagues in a meeting asking the client "Would you like me write up the notes from our discussion and send them to you?". The client's answer in the affirmative was followed that evening by the client receiving the said write-up. The second aspect of reliability is about consistency. Consultants become more trusted if the client feels he or she can rely on the consultant to hold the same opinions on a subject in different situations. Where the client suspects the consultant will be fickle in views, it becomes harder for the client to have faith in the reliability of the consultant to represent an opinion.

- *Intimacy* – the third promoter of trust is intimacy. This is about personal sharing and disclosure. An intimate relationship involves an openness of expression and information between parties as well as closeness. Intimacy is as relevant in personal relationships as it is in consulting ones. The challenge here is similar to that facing reliability. One never starts from a position of high intimacy, which means that its contribution to how trustworthy a person is perceived as is minimal. Like reliability, intimacy can grow. As consultant and client spend time in each other's company, intimacy grows. I remember arriving on a client's site (a teaching hospital) for some consultancy work. On my first visit to this site the conversation between Lynn (the primary client) and myself was cordial and pleasant, but the disclosure of intimacies went no further than reflections on the weather and my travel from our office in Glasgow. On my second visit, after being collected from the reception by Lynn, she told me she had just bumped into the doctor who had cared for her mother during her mother's six-week stay in hospital (Lynn's mother being both elderly and having dementia). The doctor and Lynn had been reflecting on her mother's modest chances of survival during the hospital treatment. This was significant personal disclosure. Lynn shared more with me on our second meeting, because she felt able to be more forthcoming having met and worked with me before.

Like reliability, the growth in intimacy can be promoted, but if attempted steps are too bold it can be scary and even unprofessional. The development of intimacy is probably best time-served and built between consultant and client through the sharing of the journey.

- *Self-interest* – this factor in the equation is the one whose presence is toxic to trust. Self-interest is where the interests of the consultant are prioritised ahead of those of the client. Here the consulting industry has done itself few favours. The term 'land and expand' describes the process of a consulting firm establishing a presence in a client organisation and then extending its commercial footprint. One of our own clients started his career as an accountant with one of the world's now prominent professional services firms. As a fledgling consultant he was told by his manager that his task was to "get yourself in there" ('there' being the client organisation) "and never leave". While it is understood that it may be possible for a consulting firm to continuously see opportunities to help and add value to a client, especially large consulting firms dealing with large clients, the deliberate pursuit of commercial opportunities by consultants raises legitimate questions around in whose best interests are these actions taken. The capability of consultants to orient work situations to suit their own priorities has been recognised – it is referred to as personal legitimising.[15] Self-interest can manifest itself in more subtle ways. For example, many clients require potential consultants to furnish references from previous clients prior to proceeding with the work. It merits reflection on whose best interest is served (that of the consulting firm or the previous client) by the use of that client's name as a reference – even with the express permission of the client.

In bringing the four ingredients of the trust equation together, it is worth remembering that all of the above relates to perception. The consultant may be very diligent in their approach to managing all of these, but it is how other key stakeholders in the project view them that matters. Beauty after all, is in the eye of the beholder. The summary of the trust equation is the ability to manage the positive construct of credibility, and the detrimental one of self-interest rests with the consultant. The two other positive components, reliability and intimacy, are likely to start low then grow throughout the project. This means that the trustworthiness of the consultant is unlikely to be at its strongest when the project is started. Many consultants have experienced the situation where they have been part-way through a project and the client has disclosed something to them that the consultant would love to have known at the start. The trust equation helps us understand why this can happen. The client needed to feel the relationship with the consultant was on a sound enough footing before this additional insight (which is often wrapped up in organisational politics and personalities) is brought into the mix.

5 Ethics and professionalism

Consulting, like social research, is not a profession in the formal sense. There is no codified body of knowledge to act as a reference point for the assessment of competence, there are no entry barriers in law to the use of the label (anyone can call themselves a consultant), and there is no ability for the body of consultants to move on accusations of malpractice against individual consultants (in the way that a lawyer can lose a practising certificate and be disbarred, or a doctor can be struck off the medical register).

In this respect, the similarity between consulting and social research should help social researchers appreciate the challenges consulting and individual consultants face in being recognised as behaving ethically and professionally.

Ethics is about standpoints. Ethical dilemmas are sometimes explained as the tension that exists between two plausible arguments. A ethical standpoint is an individual's position in respect of those arguments.[16] Ethical dilemmas associated with consulting include:

- short term versus long term
- client intellectual property versus the greater good
- honesty versus compassion
- being liked versus being respected

Reconciling these is not easy. Conceptually this is a 'wicked problem',[17] meaning there is no solution that satisfies all elements (wicked in that it resists resolution). The dilemmas are further complicated by contextual differences – as we travel we meet societies whose social norms differ, and consultants need to make calls around issues. For example, at what stage along the spectrum does being hospitable become an inducement? Should, for example, a consultant buy a client a cup of coffee? And if your answer is yes, how is that different to the consultant who takes his key clients to a music concert, or even an all-expenses-paid weekend to play golf?

Here we find the guidance on ethics in consulting offered by the ICMCI.[18] Its main qualities are that the guidance is well-researched and also designed for multicultural applicability. It covers three main areas: serving the interest of clients, transparency of representation, and professional behaviour. It provides a useful starting point for any consulting firm to build a Code of Conduct which describes its ethical stance, which it is prepared to share with its clients and use to assess the behaviour of its consultants.

Serving the interests of clients

- Engaging in projects that are only in the best interests of the client and avoiding the encouragement of unrealistic client expectations.
- Ensuring the scope, deliverables, timings and costs of consulting support are clear and agreed before starting work.
- Carrying out assignments effectively and with due care.
- Maintaining communication with the client and keeping the client adequately informed of assignment progress.
- Providing sound advice and guidance to clients.
- Refraining from inviting client's employees to consider alternative employment with them without the client's expressed permission.

Transparency of representation

- Being open and honest about qualifications, skills and expectations, and only accepting work which they are qualified to perform.
- Declaring to the client any factors that may affect their independence or objectivity, such as commission payments or other remuneration from a third party in connection with

recommendations to the client, or financial interest in any goods or services which form part of these recommendations.

- Identifying and disclosing to clients any conflicts of interest and resolving these with the client.
- Specifying and agreeing with the client any work to be subcontracted, and ensuring that subcontracted consultants abide by the same code of conduct as the consultant.

Professional behaviour

- Treating client information as confidential and respecting the confidentiality of information from any source.
- Neither taking advantage of privileged information gathered during an assignment, nor enabling others to do so.
- Acting with courtesy and respect to clients, employees and professional colleagues.
- Assuring that personal conduct does not call into question whether the consultant is a fit and proper person to carry out the profession of management consulting.

The UK's Institute of Consulting,[19] a member of ICMCI, has taken this global guidance and sharpened it for the UK context into what it refers to as a Code of Professional Conduct and Practice. The Code promotes that, in consulting practice, a consultant should:

- Put client interests first, doing whatever it takes to serve them to the highest possible standards at all times.
- Consider for each potential engagement, the possibility of it creating a conflict of interest, or the perception of such a conflict and, if such a conflict is identified, take all reasonable stops to protect the interests and confidentiality of each client.
- Act independently and objectively, and exercise professional care to establish the facts of a situation and bring to bear an informed and experienced judgement.

- Allow any action or recommendation made, if necessary, to be reviewed by one's professional peers to confirm that one has acted in a proper way.
- Continue to develop one's business consulting competencies and keep up to date with best practice.

Professionalism in any area of endeavour is dependent upon agreement of what is 'professional'. The challenge in the consulting sector is that it is outside of many consulting organisations' interests to agree what the codified body of knowledge should be. Moreover the opposite, in an unregulated market, of competitive advantage for many consulting firms is based on being different to rivals, rather than sharing the same practice. The same applies in social research. There is a range of technical skills which form the building blocks of practice (for example, survey design), but across the sector different firms offer their own proprietary approaches to assisting clients in answering research questions.

That said, there are efforts worldwide to make consulting more 'professional'. The sector has not been without criticism, especially around consulting firms being self-interested, feathering their own nests at the clients' expense, or giving valueless input. Much as the Social Research Association (SRA) seeks to improve the quality of social research in the UK, the Institute of Consulting seeks to promote quality and professional practice in the consulting field. It holds the UK franchise for the 'Certified Management Consultant' qualification, which is probably the closest the consulting profession has to a universally recognised qualification. Certified Management Consultant (CMC) is owned by the ICMCI and is based on global management consulting competencies. A minority of practising consultants are CMCs, although the number is growing. Moreover, the ICMCI competencies are used to underpin many other consulting skills development programmes, both unaccredited and as part of broader qualifications.

The ICMCI management consulting competencies can be accessed via the ICMCI website (www.cmc-global.org). These are divided into five main areas, each of which is subdivided to create a framework around which competencies expected of different levels of consulting seniority are structured. The five main areas and the subdivisions are as follows:

1.0 Client focus – 1.1 Engaging with clients, 1.2 Scoping client requirements, 1.3 Managing client interface.
2.0 Building and sustaining relationships – 2.1 Influencing, 2.2 Communication and presentations, 2.3 Facilitation, 2.4 Managing and developing others, 2.5 Partnering and networking.
3.0 Applying expertise and knowledge – 3.1 Tools and methodologies, 3.2 Applying knowledge.
4.0 Achieving sustainable results – 4.1 Planning and management, 4.2 Managing risk, 4.3 Ensuring quality, 4.4 Managing withdrawal.
5.0 Marketing capability and knowledge – 5.1 Technical expertise, 5.2 Business understanding, 5.3 Sector knowledge, 5.4 External awareness, 5.5 Business development

Social researchers will take comfort in the high degree of similarity between the competence expected of a capable social researcher and that expected of a consultant. Similarly, managers in client organisations will also notice the overlap between what makes an effective consultant and what makes an effective manager.

The next chapter looks at the outline process of consulting work, and uses this as a means of exploring some of the core consulting skills and approaches that might be useful to social researchers.

Notes

[1] There are different ways that stakeholders can be mapped. This version (power / interest) has its roots in work by Aubrey Mendelow at Kent State University, Ohio, USA in the early 1990s.

[2] The psychology and sociology of organisational change draws on a range of research insight. Of particular value is the work of Lynn Isabella, Virginia Satir, Daniel Khaneman and Chip and Dan Heath. The terms used in the text are drawn

[3] from Elizabeth Kubler-Ross' pioneering work around bereavement in her book, *On death and dying* (1969, The Macmillan Company) – the link to the organisational context being that of non-discretionary change.

[4] Further illumination of the client system can be found in *Management consultancy: boundaries and knowledge in action*, by Andrew Sturdy, Karen Handley, Timothy Clark and Robin Fincham (2010, Oxford University Press). Whereas it could be argued that there are more than four categories of 'client', the main contribution of this idea is to encourage consultants to think further than the client being a single entity.

[5] The relationship between the consulting intervention (its scope and the consulting approach) and client issue is described by Richard Newton in *Management consultancy: mastering the art of consultancy* (2012, Pearson).

[6] See www.q12gallup.com.

The idea of 'three horizons of growth' is promoted by McKinsey and Company. It is featured in *The alchemy of growth*, by Mehrdad Baghai, Stephen Coley and David White (1999, Perseus).

[7] Mimetic isomorphism, see PJ Dimaggio and WW Powell (1983), The iron cage revisited: institutional isomorphism and collective rationality in organizational fields, *American Sociological Review*, 48 (2), 147–60.

[8] The landmark text is Edgar Schein's *Process consultation* (1969, Addison-Wesley).

[9] Stephen Dubner is one of the prime movers behind Freakonomics. His interview with Traci Entel, at the time Chief Human Capital Officer at Booz and Co, is part of the Freakonomics podcast *I consult, therefore I am*, a critique of the consulting 'profession'. This podcast was launched on 28th November 2012.

[10] The series *Mary, Queen of Shops* was broadcast by BBC TV in the UK. The episode that featured the fashion boutique Comfort and Joy, based in Islington, London, was broadcast on BBC2 on 21st June 2007.

[11] Professor Tim Clark presented this profile of consulting competence in a module on Management Consulting we ran for MBA students at Durham University Business School. Tim is widely published in the field of consulting and is known for his work on consulting as the management of impressions.

[12] David Megginson and I worked together for many years developing mentoring capacity with one major not-for-profit client. David's perspective acknowledges the value of domain expertise (for example, continuous improvement techniques) as a foundation for capable process consulting.

[13] See David Maister, Charles Green, and Robert Galford, *The trusted advisor* (2000, Free Press). The focus of David Maister's career as an academic was the professions, with the implication that his insights into subjects like trust are oriented toward activities like consulting.

[14] For further insight into the trust equation, see www.trustedadvisor.com.

[15] See Simon Haslam's *Personal legitimising: a substantive grounded theory in the context of small consultancy firms* (1999, University of Strathclyde PhD thesis).

[16] There are several sources of insight into organisational ethics. Information on the Institute of Business Ethics can be found at www.ibe.org.uk. Also ICMCI Academic Fellow, Dr Joe O'Mahoney is recognised for his work on ethics in the consulting arena – see his book, *Management consultancy*, co-written with Calvert Markham (2nd edn, 2013, Oxford University Press).

[17] The origin of the term 'wicked problem' in this context goes back to 1967 and an editorial written by C West Churchman in *Management Science*.

[18] See www.cmc-global.org.

[19] See www.iconsulting.org.uk.

3

THE CONSULTING PROCESS

Chapter 3 is based on the consulting process and the sequence of typical activities from the beginning of a consulting project to the end. It builds upon the ideas in the previous chapter, particularly how consultants add value and the different types of consulting approach.

The consulting process will resonate with many social researchers, especially those commissioning social research work and people who are contract researchers, as there are many parallels between the life of social research projects and that of consulting projects.

- *Section 1* draws attention to the effectiveness of a consulting process, which is as much about the client as it is about the consultant.
- *Section 2* introduces the 'consulting cycle' as an outline structure for the consulting process. Having provided the structure of the consulting cycle, the remainder of the chapter homes in on specific areas of the cycle, and in particular where the consulting perspective might be of use to social researchers.
- *Section 3* talks about assignment intimacy.
- *Section 4* explores the value of logic in the design of consulting projects.
- *Section 5* looks at the role of management models in consulting work.
- *Section 6* looks at the core consulting skill of interviewing.

- *Section 7* builds on social research's understanding of data issues and suggests how data can be developed into insight in consulting work.
- *Section 8* looks at how logic applies to the way in which the results and recommendations from consulting work can be framed.
- *Section 9*, titled 'The prestige', talks about how the results of consulting work might be presented in order to demonstrate and realise value for the client.

1 Good clients

It is easy, as a consultant, to assume the responsibility for the success of a project. If the arrangement with a client is a commercial one, the onus is perhaps even more obvious. Calvert Markham, who helped establish the International Council for Management Consulting Institutes (ICMCI), expressed the following view:[1]

> When consultants are publicly criticised, it is often not for their performance, but for the quality of the project for which they have been engaged. The introduction of initiatives and formulation of projects is a joint venture between consultants and their clients, and it needs excellence of performance from both parties. Not only do we need excellent consultants, but also excellent clients.

The point that Calvert makes is one of a shared duty and reminds consultants of the importance of helping clients be 'excellent clients', even though they are investing in the consultants to generate value.

My consulting firm, FMR Research, was fortunate to be nominated to represent the UK's consulting sector at the Constantinus International consulting awards.[2] At the awards, leading consulting projects from around the world were showcased, and a winner chosen by a panel comprising representatives of the world's management consulting institutes. We came sixth (which we were delighted with). The project for which we were nominated was an organisational review of the Scottish Institute for Residential Childcare (SIRCC).[3] While the methodology we adopted was sound, involving one-to-one interviews with each member of the organisation using a topic guide co-developed with the client, which focused on 11 factors deemed strategically important, the success of this project was more a testament to the investment by the client than it was to the consulting approach. SIRCC invested fully in the process with a commitment of resources, time and openness to the process which took the work far from a team of consultants 'doing something' to a client organisation.

As we will explore in the next chapter, being able to challenge how a client sees a situation, and facilitate the introduction of fresh perspectives, is fundamental to what consulting is about. Where clients aren't as naturally open and contributory as SIRCC in the above example, the consultant's finesse is about how she or he can provide the appropriate challenge to the client, while simultaneously keeping the client committed to and excited about the overall success of the work. The cohesion that comes from client and consultant agreeing and sharing goals from the project needs to be stronger than the force of challenge in the consulting process.

2 The consulting cycle… and its implications

The idea of the consulting cycle was promoted by Lippitt and Lippitt in 1986.[4] It provides a useful general framework for thinking about the stages from inception to completion of consulting work. While the original consulting cycle has six stages, these are not hard and fast categories; the number of stages and the content of each may change from project to project. And for social researchers accustomed to either commissioning or delivering social research projects, rather than give a full description of the consulting cycle, we will concentrate on the potential pinch points or areas of contention in consulting work.

Figure 3.1: The consulting cycle

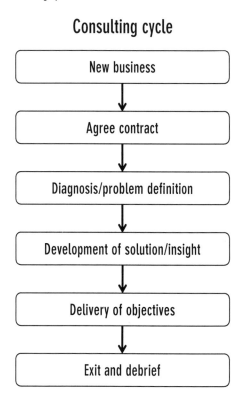

Consulting cycle

New business

↓

Agree contract

↓

Diagnosis/problem definition

↓

Development of solution/insight

↓

Delivery of objectives

↓

Exit and debrief

An overview of each of the six stages follows:

New business – this can come from various directions. From a consulting perspective, the three most useful steps in moving from an outline opportunity to securing new business are probably: 1) giving the potential client confidence in your/your team's abilities and trustworthiness; 2) demonstrating a sufficient understanding of the client's context, which might lead to a proposed approach which is distinctive (in a good way); and 3) showing a genuine appetite for doing the work. In addition, the overall value of the consulting work to the client is likely to be enhanced if the consultant is able to grasp early on in the consulting cycle why the client wants this particular consulting work carried out.

While a consultant and a social researcher might both be scrutinised by a prospective client in terms of methodological competency and personal fit, one difference between the two is that consulting is possibly less defined and more abstract as a form of intervention than social research. This means that the client may be more apprehensive in the selection of a consultant. This is represented in the consulting literature as consulting being about impression management; it has been said that the greatest competence of a consultant is the ability to appear competent.[5] Consultants have long appreciated the merits of being able to meet prospective clients in advance of preparing proposals, from the dual perspectives of seeking to create a favourable impression and also to learn more about the project, but the current fashion towards objective assessment and de-personalised approaches in procurement practice has tempered this somewhat.

New contract – the two main considerations for a consultant are very similar to that of a social research project at new contract stage. These are: 1) agreeing the scope of the intervention in terms of time, cost and project objectives; and 2) agreeing the project management protocols – how the consultant and the client will work together and manage the successful execution of the project.

The processes by which a consulting contract is agreed are also very similar to that for many social research contracts. Consultants will often submit a written proposal, the depth of which is commensurate with the value of the prospective contract. The proposal then forms the basis for the commissioning meeting with the client, should the proposal be accepted. At the commissioning meeting, the scope of the proposed intervention and consulting approach are usually discussed with the client, and may be subject to refinement.

Where the scope of work is tightly defined it can be difficult for a consultant to demonstrate differentiation from his or her competitors. One way that can help is if the consultant is able to give the client additional options and ideas around what to do in the project. As options, as distinct from the core work, they don't detract from how the client framed the work – the choice of whether to include them in the project or not remains in the hands of the client.

Diagnosis and problem definition – a consulting project is similar to a social research project in that there is an initial period of divergence during which data are sourced and the foundation of understanding built, followed by a convergent phase where insight is sharpened and recommendations crystallised. There is a fine line between continuing to cast the net for information wide, on the basis that until you see the data you are not aware of what is important or not, and being structured and efficient from the outset. There is no hard and fast guidance here, but be aware that each extra piece of information embraced (be that an additional interview carried out or each additional report analysed) absorbs project resources to acquire and digest it.

Development of solutions from insight – one of the main challenges in consulting work is 'scope creep'. Scope creep exists when the scope and scale of a consulting project extends from its original specification. Either the client seeks extra work to be conducted within the bounds of the original contract, or the consultant extends the amount of work involved within the contract's fee structure. There can be many reasons why scope creep happens, many of them positive, but the main challenge is about how the consultant deals with it.

There are conflicting perspectives on how one should respond to scope creep. On one side of the see-saw is the recognition that extra unpaid work reduces the profitability of the project. The consultant can legitimately point to the project specification agreed at 'new contract' stage and suggest that any extra work beyond the terms of the original contract will be charged as an extra. On the other side, the goodwill the consultant creates by willingly doing extra work for no extra charge is likely to be the most cost-effective marketing he or she will ever do – the most powerful marketing collateral for a consultant is usually their perceived performance in delivering projects. As stated above, there is no hard and fast recommendation on how to respond to and capitalise on scope creep, but it may be useful for a consultant to anticipate the likelihood of this on a contract and build the economic model with sufficient capacity / resilience to cover it.

One consulting firm I researched felt their scope-creep contingency was around 20% of a project's value.

Delivery of objectives – no surprises! As the consulting project nears its conclusion, it is useful to share insights and the implications with the primary client ahead of producing draft and final reports. The purpose of this is twofold: first, to sense-check findings to date; second, to socialise the implications of the research with those who will be affected by them. On occasion, consultants have run 'findings workshops' with stakeholders ahead of draft report stage to accomplish this. We go further into the presentation of project outputs to clients in 'The prestige'.

Exit – Lippitt and Lippitt's idea of a 'consulting cycle' suggests that the process is circular, and the consultant will probably move onto another client project as this project comes to an end. As a consulting project comes to an end, it should be acknowledged and celebrated.

It is helpful for the consultant to leave the door open. This means for the client to feel able to continue the relationship without feeling pressured to do so by the client. Consultants have little difficulty in identifying opportunities for further commercial opportunities when working on a project, and in many respects have earned a reputation for such. Hard-fought-for trust is easily lost should the consultant behave in a self-interested manner and manufacture the ability to extend billable work beyond the initial terms of reference.

The richest source of learning for consultants is their clients, and overstepping the mark in respect of the client's intellectual property is a common transgression, whether this be using the client as a reference for future work without permission, or using the client project as a case study.

3 Project intimacy

Part of the discussion between the consultant and client, perhaps at commissioning but certainly before the work starts, is 'project intimacy'. This is about how much or how little your client expects to see you during the consulting project.

For three weeks, in the summer of 2012, I took a position in a consulting project in Belgrade, joining a team put together by one of the German consulting firms on work focused on helping prepare Serbia for its entry to the EU. The work itself went well, and the team accomplished what was expected of it. My three-week contribution represented a small element over a fuller two-year programme. The main learning for me, though, related to the expected style of the consulting work, not the content. My client expected me to be on site with them every day over the duration of the project, to start work at the same time as the rest of the workforce and finish at the same time as everyone else. Lunch would be taken with the other team members, as would coffee breaks. In other words, the client expected a high degree of intimacy. While this may seem a reasonable expectation, it is not the way my firm typically works on social research and consulting projects. Our usual way of working is to agree a scope of work with the client then, over the agreed time period, carry out some work on site (for example interviews, focus groups and workshops), but the majority of it off site (desk research, primary research with other parties, and writing).

This approach enables us to flex the intensity of effort as the project requirements ebb and flow, for example there is often a degree of downtime on a project between setting up interviews and conducting them. In these gentler periods on a project, we would devote time to other projects and matters like business development. Conversely, the intense periods in projects would be met by intense effort from ourselves, going way beyond the nine-to-five and straying into evenings and weekend working as appropriate. Working out of sight of the client enables us to manage time effectively and without a great deal of scrutiny. Many tasks on a project can be performed equally well, if not better, off site.

The problem I faced in Belgrade was that I did not have the conversation about the client's expectation of how the consulting work was to be conducted ahead of getting started. I carried an assumption into the project which was unwarranted and led to an awkward discussion on the second day, when I suggested that the preparatory writing I needed to do could be just as capably executed from the desk in my apartment as it would be on the client's premises.

For those working as internal consultants, the problem of project intimacy is complicated by the recognition that it is difficult for the consultant to 'escape' from the client premises. Internal consultants are usually on site and accessible even if they are not working on that client's particular project. However, boundaries between the consultant's time and other priorities, and the client's wishes in terms of access to and control over the consultant, are more capably managed if there is a discussion about them at commissioning stage.

4 Logic in project design

4.1 The pyramid principle

Many years ago, one of my academic colleagues introduced me to the work of Barbara Minto. I still feel that Minto's book, *The pyramid principle*, is one of the most valuable texts to the practising consultant.[6] Minto built her reputation as the coach to the McKinsey consulting team before doing similar for PA Consulting and subsequently branching out on her own.

This section is devoted to Barbara Minto's vocational focus: the better application of logic in consulting work. Logic has two main applications in consulting work. The first is in project design and the other is in project reporting. We will look at each in turn. Before we do that it is important to appreciate Minto's perspective on logic and how ideas can (and should) be organised. I have heard the pyramid principle described as a discourse in Vulcan logic, meaning that it is a deep dive founded upon entirely rational principles and a premise that prizes the power of logic over the power of emotion – the reference to 'Vulcan' being Mr Spock of Star Trek, whose appetite for understanding was rooted totally in logical arguments with no emotion.

Minto's approach to logic, as the title of her book implies, is that ideas should have a pyramid shape. The top of the pyramid is the overall, main idea and the levels below are the sub-ideas / components of the main idea. In the design of pyramids of logic there are three rules:

- Ideas at any level in the pyramid are summaries of the ideas grouped below.
- Ideas in a group should be the same kind of idea.
- Ideas in a group should be logically ordered.

A pyramid can have many levels. Providing these rules are adhered to, Barbara Minto gives us the means to organise arrays of data or ideas in ways that make logical sense. This logic is of great value in planning consulting projects and communicating their output.

4.2 Logic in project design

I approach consulting projects from the paradigm of inductive research, that is to say I prefer to wait for a full immersion into data before I seek a theoretical interpretation. I found this application of logic to consulting work conceptually challenging, therefore, and somewhat at odds with my social research apprenticeship.

Logic in project design means, at a very early stage in a consulting project's life (even at bid stage), that the consultant builds a hypothesis around the phenomenon under investigation. This means that there is a clear understanding of the problem to be resolved and, from that, the activities necessary (scope, scale and sequence) that will be undertaken to resolve the hypothesis. That hypothesis, based on the assumptions about the work involved, will govern the design of the project, the sequencing of activities and the allocation of resources. As an experienced *grounded theory* researcher, I belonged to the 'it is a capital mistake to theorise before one has data' school,[7] but I have come to appreciate the value of initial theory building, using partial data and assumptions to make a start with project design.

The main benefit of using a logical approach to developing a working hypothesis is that it helps project resources to be used efficiently: the most expensive component of most consulting operations is human resources, and once a person's time has been spent on an activity, it cannot be re-spent. Expressions like 'burning the budget' abound in the consulting sector to describe activity which is fruitless. When a budget is being burned, resources are being consumed but without valuable outputs. Consulting projects ought to be an exercise in efficiency, and the pyramid principle allows expensive and finite resources to be efficiently oriented. The second benefit is in communication. If there is an initial hypothesis, the consultant can test their understanding with the client. It is far better for the consultant to learn that the assumptions about the project are misplaced at the beginning of the work, than at the end.

The way to build a hypothesis using the pyramid principle is as follows:

- Identify the main deliverable for the consulting work (the top of the pyramid); this is what the consultant is commissioned to deliver.
- List all the activities that the consulting project might cover in order to fulfil the objective.
- Cluster these together in groups (look for themes between the activities).
- Delete activities that are beyond the scope / control of the project.
- Link activities together and build the pyramid, with smaller activities sitting under the themes and the themes sitting under the main objective / deliverable.
- Put time and cost estimates against each of the activities.
- Sense-check the hypothesis. First, does the hypothesis pass the MECE test? meaning are the activities *mutually exclusive* (no duplication or overlaps), and are they *collectively exhaustive* (no missing ingredients or gaps). Second, is the sum of the resources needed for the project, and the time to complete it, within the client's expectations of budget and deadline?

Here is an example. In an episode of the TV series, *Mary, Queen of Shops*, retail specialist Mary Portas works with London fashion boutique Comfort and Joy.[8] Knowing that the business is struggling, Mary makes her initial assessment by visiting the boutique. This intelligence gathering is sufficient for Mary to form her hypothesis and build her plan for the project. The main issue in her opinion was the business's image. Mary felt the boutique looked tired and its current image failed to communicate Comfort and Joy's competitive appeal: that it had its own clothes designer and products as well as stocking other lines and brands. Within the deliverable of giving Comfort and Joy a new image, Mary felt there was work to be done on branding, physical layout and product merchandising. Within the branding theme were three activities: 1) customer perception work around the current name; 2) coming up with a new name; 3) visual identity around the new name. Within the physical environment theme were three activities: 1) opening up the back room and making it part of the shop; 2) removing the central display unit that divided the main shop's space; 3) re-decorating the shop, inside and out. Under the product merchandising theme there were two activities: 1) window display; and 2) stock presentation within the shop. This logic pyramid was the basis for Mary's successful execution of the work. In creating the pyramid she did not use the terms 'logic' or 'hypothesis' – clients don't need the jargon to get the picture. Mary also excluded one possible component of business image from her hypothesis – the physical location of the shop – on the basis that this could not be changed.

Here is a second example. My firm was presented with an opportunity to help a research organisation with its restructuring and relocation programme. The 'hypothesis' was that, given the constraints of time and budget, the focus of the consulting intervention should engage external support to help its leaders work with their colleagues and teams through what was going to be a challenging change for many. The building blocks of this support were: three half-day workshops to cover the concepts of change leadership; psychometric profiling to enable leaders and teams to learn about their personalities in respect of change; the creation of an intranet site populated with change and leadership tools to help the research organisation with the change process; and the creation of action learning groups to help leaders to work together on problem solving as the change journey unfolded. Excluded from the project logic were the consultants' ability to select the leaders (or recruit new ones for the firm), and to work directly with the bulk of the staff.

The initial hypothesis is a working one, meaning that as data change, so might the assumptions that underpinned the hypothesis. For instance, in the above example, the project might reassign resources to support more action learning activity and reduce the workshop element from three to two half-days. The project design, in the form of an evolving hypothesis, is able to flex such that project resources can be re-focused as appropriate to represent valuable activity and generate positive outputs.

It is not uncommon for a larger consulting project to start with a scoping study, which is a discrete and initial piece of work whose aim is to generate the data to enable the hypothesis for the main work to be created, so that resources can be used efficiently and also effectively in the resolution of an accurately diagnosed issue. Even a scoping is likely to benefit from an initial and hypothetical articulation of how the resources in the scoping study are to be deployed.

5 Management models

Just as a social researcher will have a research paradigm underpinning their work in a research project, so a consultant is likely to have a management model or framework at the core of how they propose to generate and interpret data in the course of a consulting assignment. There are very many management concepts and frameworks available, with more created every year. Within the not-for-distributed-profit arena, stakeholder mapping, business model canvas, value chain analysis, employee engagement, social return on investment and options appraisal have garnered popularity. Below are some of the perspectives that may influence a consultant's choice of model.

- *Add value* – the main reason why consultants should use management ideas is that they draw on the insights of others and contribute to a more effective way of organising project resources, analysing and synthesising data and generating insight. The use of management ideas in a consulting project requires the consultant to be knowledgeable about the concept and confident in applying it. The grasp needs to be more substantial than that of a lecturer being two pages of the textbook ahead of his students. The client feeling confident in the consultant's abilities is usually central to the client and consultant being able to work together towards excellent results.

- *Own the toolbox* – if the hammer is the only tool in a handyman's toolbox, every job had better involve a nail. Ideally, a consultant's toolbox is more broadly equipped than a single tool (or he or she is likely to treat every project as if it was a nail),[9] backed by the capability to know what tool to pick out in each different situation and how to use it in an accomplished manner.

- *Less is more* – with such an abundance of choice, it is tempting for a consultant to flex their conceptual muscles and use an array of management ideas and frameworks on a single assignment. Be warned: such enthusiasm is usually misplaced and serves to confuse the client or, worse, create the impression that the consultant has merely digested the contents of an MBA primer. A clearer understanding of the landscape under investigation will usually lead to one or two front runners, and using these only will often help with a logical and transparent project design – benefiting client and consultant alike.

- *Management is fashionable* – the choice of management models used in a consulting assignment has a symbolic element as well as a functional one. The management thinking a consultant brings into a project is equivalent to the style of clothes the consultant wears. Some management ideas are on trend, while others are dependable though unremarkable, and still others are passé. From a UK perspective, the consulting sector has seen ideas like Investors in People, Best Value, and Lean ascend to heights of popularity, only to later decline. It is the consultant's call how contemporary they wish to be, and often the client will declare enough to give the consultant a steer on the type of approach likely to find favour, at pre-contract stage. Few consultants have ever built capital out of SWOT (Strengths, Weaknesses, Opportunities, Threats) analysis[10] – which is no reflection on the utility of the concept (if used appropriately) but a recognition that practically every client already knows about it, meaning the consultant is adding nothing in terms of original thought to the client in suggesting it as an approach.

- *Create the IP* – the management consulting sector is richly populated by management concepts and intellectual property (IP) created by consultants themselves, for example Boston Consulting Group's eponymous matrix[11] and McKinsey's Organizational Health Index.[12] Done well, these proprietary approaches help to position the consultants as different from their direct competitors. It also helps the consulting team to develop specific expertise as the world's most experienced people in their technique, and to set off a virtuous circle where they deploy the approach on an ever-increasing number of clients while simultaneously further developing their understanding and skill.

6 Interviews

Interviewing is one of the core activities in many areas of consulting, as it is in many social research projects. This section aims to highlight particular areas of practice which are perhaps different to the way that interviews may be approached in social research. Here is a summary of general guidelines around interviewing that have served consultants well, to augment good practice in social research interviews.

- *Start with the primary client* – a consultant's relationship with the primary client is often key to the success of the project. In the data-gathering process, the initial views of the primary client help the consultant and primary client share the common ground at project inception. Consulting work also typically benefits from the early input of the ultimate client (or stakeholders more senior to the primary client), as these people usually hold significant sway in terms of how the results of the consulting work may be implemented.

- *Ask the primary client to set up other interviews*– in situations where the primary client either knows the interviewee well and/or has organisational seniority over them, the primary client is better placed than the consultant to tee up the interview, or even arrange it. Consultants, for the most part, are an inconvenience to most people's working lives, and in many respects a threat (as they herald change and all the uncertainty that it carries). The primary client's positional power and relationship credentials can help smooth the way.

- *… but make it easy for the primary client* – in these days of Doodle and shared access diaries, scheduling interviews is far less of an administrative burden than it used to be. Consultants can also help by drafting letters of introduction or emails for the primary client to send out.

- *Be clear about the 'why'* – consulting interviews usually work better if the client (intermediate, proscribed, and so on) appreciates the reason for the interruption to their lives: why the consultant wants the interview and what the consultant is keen to learn. In some social research situations, the reason for an interview may be shielded from the interviewee for fear of it biasing the responses. In consulting, interviews are more about developing and deepening dialogue, and key to the building of trust in this respect is openness.

- *Topic guide up front* – following the above sentiment, consulting interviews tend to give the interviewee as much of a 'heads-up' as possible about the purpose of the interview. Usually this is in the form of a topic guide with, as maximum, a handful of lines of enquiry. Having the topic guide in advance gives interviewees the opportunity to come to the interview prepared. In the interview, each of these lines of enquiry provides a platform for discussion, with the consultant able to probe and encourage the client as appropriate.

- *Agree some ground rules* – part of the preliminary work around the interview includes the rules of engagement, especially the bounds of confidentiality. In some situations, consultants may ask that the interviewees mention no-one by name; in extreme cases not even job roles are sought, for fear of these individuals being identified as a result. Ground rules agreed, and adhered to, help with building rapport.

- *Future orientation and client ownership* – the tone of most consulting interviews tends to be future-oriented. Discussions about the present (what happens now) and the past are often paths into the future ('what could…'). In this way the consultant can help to avoid any disclosure around less than healthy practice in the client organisation becoming a witch hunt, and steer it to being more about co-created opportunities, using the wisdom from the client system as a major ingredient.

- *Take notes with permission* – for most people, taking notes in an interview is a necessity. Memories are rarely capable of hanging onto the detail and texture of what is shared over a 60-minute period. Two factors merit consideration. First, take keypoint notes only. In that way, the consultant is less likely to become disengaged from the interview. Body posture and eye contact are vital for the client to sense that the consultant is 'in the room' with them. After the interview, go back over the notes and add the extra parts (using a different coloured pen) while they are still fresh. Second, a consultant should never write anything down that she or he would not be prepared to share with a client. In the development of a trust-based relationship the consultant has only one answer to give when the interviewee says "Sorry, I didn't think to make notes of our discussion, but I notice you did. Can I have a copy of yours please". I have witnessed one car-crash of an interview when two bank managers referred detrimentally, in their scribbles, to the client they were interviewing, thinking the client would never see the words.

- *Taping is pretty much a no, no* – in the social research setting, recording interviews with the expressed permission of the interviewee is integral to many data generation techniques. The general perspective in the consulting field is that note-taking is fine, but taping discussions helps neither a sense of trust nor the openness of opinion. And don't even think about taping without permission unless the consulting project is covert surveillance.

- *Facts are friends* – it can be difficult to upset the flow of a discussion but, while sentiment is useful, specifics are essential. Without specific details too much is left to the consultant to infer or interpret. There is, for example, a massive difference between 10% and 50% in size increase of an organisation, whose director said in the interview she wanted to grow the organisation this year. In the interview, the consultant can acknowledge the sentiment and use it to explore the specifics: "that's interesting you'd like to grow the organisation this year, do you have a target in mind…?".

- *Appreciate the value of people's contributions and leave the door open* – every client probably has something else that he or she could be doing, other than speaking with the consultant. As well as appreciating the interviewee's time and contribution, a consultant may also end the interview by seeking permission to re-contact the interviewee at a later date, should the consultant have further questions. A positive answer from the client here (very, very few interviewees refuse) legitimises the consultant getting back in touch at a later date, and pretty much guarantees answers to the follow-up questions they ask.

- *The Columbo technique* – many social researchers already use the Columbo technique in their interviews. Named after the 1970s American raincoated detective,[13] the technique involves deliberately not asking the key or sensitive question in the interview, but waiting until the interview is finished. It's the 'just one more thing' prefix as the interviewee walks the consultant back to reception or out of the office into the daylight. Asking questions when people's guards are down sometimes helps. There is an ethical question for the consultant to answer, namely the justification for what some might see as subterfuge. The levers of influence can be just as effective if deployed for selfish means as they can for wholesome ones. There may be a distinction here between the social research approach (where information given after the interview is finished may not be regarded as data) and the consulting approach which is more likely to take the more liberal view that everything is data and potentially helpful.

7 Data to insight

Social researchers are usually deft at handling data, numerical or otherwise. Below are some of the main considerations when it comes to data in consulting projects.

- *Make estimates* – job candidates interested in careers with the big consulting houses are usually subject to a multi-faceted selection process.[14] Competition for places is high, and the consulting firms recognise that the future of their brands and their prosperity pretty much depends on the talent they recruit and nurture. During the interview the candidate might be asked a specific data question to which he or she is very unlikely to know the answer, for example, how many red cars are there in Greater Manchester? What the interview panel are typically looking for is not the proximity to the actual value, but a logical way of approaching the problem which will lead quickly to a reasonable approximation. In this example, a factor like the size of the UK population (which most candidates will have a strong enough feel for) as a starting point is melded with the proportion of the UK population resident in Greater Manchester, and then the number of households in the UK, car ownership per (urban) household, the proportion of cars that are red, and so forth, will come into play. A consultant will need to be able to make calls on the direction of a project based on imperfect information – the timescale and the budget is likely to make thorough analysis impossible in every case. Getting a feel for where to look first, and what to de-prioritise quickly and efficiently, helps a project move further, quicker.

- *Know the assumptions* – the power of numbers, especially percentages, to influence opinion is well understood in behavioural economics – represented, for example, by the cognitive bias of 'anchoring'. 'Curiosity' is a more valuable watchword around data, than 'trust'. In practice, when looking at results, forecasts, revenue projections and so on, pay particular attention to the assumptions at the foundation of the data, much in the way that a social researcher will be curious to know the research method behind any findings or results. Looking at the assumptions rather than taking the data at face value helps generate understanding, and reduces the risk of unnecessary confrontation where the data needs to be agreed or disagreed with.

- *Look for the vital few* – management consultant Joseph Juran popularised the *Pareto principle* in management circles. Also known as the 80:20 rule, the Pareto principle states that around 80% of the outputs come from 20% of the inputs. This skew between cause and effect was first noted by Italian economist Vilfredo Pareto (he validated the 80:20 rule by showing that the majority of land in Italy was owned by a minority of the population, and that the bulk of the pea crop in his garden came from the 'vital few' of his plants). Juran's guidance is valuable – an 80% solution is usually easier to manage than a 100% solution, as the former only needs attention to 20% of the inputs. Just as the manager of a supermarket will know the minority of the products that generate the bulk of the sales revenue or account for the biggest element of inventory problems, grasping the vital few leads to very efficient use of resources. Client organisations have finite bandwidth (capacity to comprehend and capacity to deliver) which means that the most valuable consulting usually focuses on those items which have a disproportionately high impact for the client.

- *What's the story?* – accepting that correlation doesn't mean causality, also accepting that people display a disposition to 'tidy up' complexity (hindsight bias), and that people attract information which supports their beliefs (confirmation bias), the continual questioning about what the data are saying, as a project progresses, is useful. It is costly to conduct research and to carry out analyses. It is helpful to prioritise lines of enquiry and analyses that relate to the needs of the consulting project. By keeping abreast of what the messages are from the data, additional research and further analyses can be well focused on helping important questions to get answered. In practice, don't commit the entire research and analysis budget on day one, as it is really difficult to predict with full accuracy what data are required and what analyses should be conducted. Plan sufficient research and analysis to get started, and use that as a basis for refining the focus as the work progresses.

8 Logic in presentation

Barbara Minto's work on logic in a consulting context (see *section 4*, above) extends to how consultants frame the output of their work and present their ideas and recommendations to clients. Minto's view is that too many consultants lack the ability to communicate project results powerfully and cohesively. The same three rules for logic in project design apply to logic in recommendations. The main message should be the most prominent, and this should be supported by messages at the lower levels of the pyramid, as appropriate. The order in which the lower-order messages are reported also needs to follow a logic, for if this logic is not clear the client is left wondering about the basis on which the findings have been prioritised, and the consultant has unwittingly succeeded in distracting the client's attention from the core message.

Here is an example. This consultancy project has sought to investigate the UK's decline as a manufacturing location. The project report concludes with the following findings:

The causes of the UK's decline as a manufacturing location are principally as follows:

1. UK wage rates are substantially higher than most other places in the world.
2. Land costs are higher in the UK than they are in many other countries, especially developing nations.
3. The UK has a highly developed regulatory and health and safety framework, which adds to enterprise cost.
4. There are comparatively few manufacturing cluster areas in the UK, meaning a general lack of manufacturing expertise and capacity.
5. There is increasing competition from other nations as manufacturing locations, especially in Asia and eastern Europe.
6. The UK economy has been shifting to the service sector.

While these findings may be accurate, their presentation fails the pyramid logic test. A more impactive way of presenting the same message could be as follows:

The UK's decline as a manufacturing location is the result of three factors – cost, capacity and competition:

1. *Costs* – the UK's wage rates, land costs and regulatory framework renders it comparatively unattractive as an international manufacturing location.
2. *Capacity* – the UK's shift to a service sector economy and its relative lack of manufacturing cluster areas has resulted in low levels of capacity to support manufacturing enterprise.
3. *Competition* – other nations, especially in Asia and eastern Europe, are becoming increasingly attractive manufacturing locations.

This presents the data as a three-level pyramid with three main ingredients, rather than as a list of six factors. A list of three is easier to remember than a list of six, and the three main ingredients represent a level of synthesis absent in the list of six.

Social researchers appreciate the importance of keeping messages from data within the limits of the data's reliability and validity. Applications of the pyramid principle should also respect the same. Data, however, can benefit from a more capable organisation for the benefits of communication and comprehension, without it needing to be subject to a cavalier treatment.

9 The Prestige

The Prestige is like the punch line in a magician's trick[15] – that flourish or essence of theatre that adds sparkle to the technical proficiency of the illusion. This section discusses how consultants can present their project conclusions or recommendations, and how the technical proficiency the consultants have brought to the project can be brought more to life with greater impact.

- *Use S-C-S to frame the message* – Situation – Complication – Solution is a three-step approach to introducing a message, based on Barbara Minto's work.[16] The process works as follows: start by saying something uncontestable about the situation the consulting project has addressed – the keypoint being that anything contestable early on in a presentation or message stands a chance of alienating the audience or distracting them from what comes next. Follow this by the Complication, which is a distillation of why this study is important or difficult. The complication serves to emphasise the gravity of the task and build up the importance of the consulting work. The third step is the Solution, which is the output of the consultancy work and a summary of the value the consulting work has provided. Note, the S-C-S approach can be used equally well for sales presentations at pre-contract stage, framing the introductory section to consulting proposals as well as consulting reports.

During the S-C-S process, it is very helpful to remind the audience of the purpose of the consulting project, and what the agreed deliverables were. This helps to anchor whatever the conclusions or recommendations cover.

- *Keep the main thing, the main thing. That's the main thing* – this Zig Ziglar sentiment reinforces the importance of making sure the main findings are shared with the audience, when the audience is at its most attentive.[17] – right up front. Circling back to Barbara Minto's guidance around the pyramid principle (see *section 4*), start the content with the top of the pyramid (the 'main thing'), then use pyramid logic to organise and sequence the rest of the content.

- *Visualise for impact* – can you show the implications in a killer graph? An extrapolation from the current position is that the recommendations are followed, compared to the 'do nothing' option? Can you summarise the key messages in an infographic?

- *Demonstrate value* – the client will have invested time and (probably) money in the consulting project, and the quest to deliver value should never be far from the consultant's mind. Pick this up directly and articulate how the consulting work has delivered value for the client. To do this, there is likely to be the need for interpolations and extrapolations (with assumptions), but this mindset will keep the reporting of the consulting work focused on the client's main issue.

- *Mind your language* – pay attention to the tone of conclusions and recommendations. 'Deficit' language can be incendiary and cloud a client's willingness to embrace the message. Most ideas can be flipped, for example shortcomings can be reframed as areas of potential or having scope for further development.

- *One thought: two styles* – one useful insight from the area of information comprehension is the value of expressing one thought in two ways. First, give the headline in a short and succinct way, two to four words. Then, provide a fuller explanation. There is a temptation to combine the two, especially in written reports, but that is more likely to reflect the shortcomings of each style rather than the strengths. Practically, the one thought: two styles approach can mean a tabular format with two columns, using bold and non-bold text or sub-heads and supporting narrative. This very bullet-pointed list serves to illustrate.

- *Show the likely returns, if further investment is recommended* – often, consulting work results in recommendations for the client to make additional investments, for example, the setting up of new systems or the creation of a new post. Where recommendations encourage the client to make extra investments, quantify the likely positive impact for the client, and use a multiplier of at least three (ideally more), as clients have learned that things usually cost more and/or deliver less than planned.

- *Keep your hands out of the client's pocket* – one sure way to undermine the goodwill that the consultant has generated, by working diligently on the client's project, is to suggest to the client that she or he commission the consultant to carry out further work. It is likely that a consultant with a finger on the pulse will see plenty of opportunities as to how the client's situation can be further improved with additional investment. By all means, the consultant could draw the client's attention to these, but the line between the consultant helping the client, and being perceived by the client as self-interested, is a fine one. We introduced the subject of consulting ethics in *Chapter 2,* and it is a recurring theme in this book, especially where consulting skills relate to methods of influence.

The next chapter looks at the techniques at a consultant's disposal to help challenge prevailing perspectives, as skills that are pretty much universally applicable throughout the consulting cycle.

Notes

[1] Calvert Markham is an ICMCI Academic Fellow. His comment about good clients is sourced from the article, Consultancy – a fashion industry? in Management Accounting (April 1997).

[2] The Constantinus International awards are the annual global showcase of management consulting projects. Entries come from around the world, each entry being a nomination from a national Institute of Management Consulting (in the UK this is the Institute of Consulting).

[3] The Scottish Institute for Residential Childcare is now CELCIS, an organisation with a wider remit around looked-after children, see www.celcis.org.

[4] See Gordon Lippitt and Ronald Lippitt, *The consulting process in action* (1986, Wiley). See also Julie Hodges, *Consultancy, organizational development and change: a practical guide for delivery value*, (2017, Kogan Page).

[5] This phrase was offered by Professor Tim Clark in a module on Management Consulting we were running for MBA students at Durham University Business School.

[6] See Barbara Minto, *The pyramid principle: logic in writing and thinking* (3rd edn, 2008, Financial Times/Prentice Hall). For more information on Barbara Minto see www.barbaraminto.com.

[7] This quote is from Arthur Conan Doyle's Sherlock Holmes in *A scandal in Bohemia* (1891).

[8] The episode of *Mary, Queen of Shops* that featured the fashion boutique Comfort and Joy, based in Islington, London, was broadcast on BBC2 on 21st June, 2007.

[9] This is known as the 'Law of the instrument', as popularised by Abraham Maslow with the sentiment 'if all you have is a hammer, then everything looks like a nail', from his book, *Psychology of science* (1966, Chicago Gateway).

[10] SWOT analysis is accredited to Albert Humphrey, who was involved in research at Stanford University in the 1960s and 1970s, although Humphrey himself never laid claim to the idea.

[11] The Boston Consulting Group (BCG) matrix, encourages organisations to look at the balance across their portfolio of activities, using the constructs of relative market share as a proxy for the competitive strength of each part of the portfolio and market growth rate to illuminate the future prospects for the markets in question. The matrix popularised terms like 'cash cow' and 'dog', which are widely used in strategic management. The creation of the idea goes back to 1970 and is attributed to Bruce Henderson, founder of the BCG.

[12] McKinsey Organizational Health Index, see www.mckinsey.com.

[13] Columbo was an American television series which starred Peter Falk as a homicide detective with the LAPD. It ran for ten seasons between 1968 and 1978.

[14] Probably the most accessible, valuable insight is provided in Victor Cheng's book, *Case interview: a former McKinsey interviewer reveals how to get multiple job offers in consulting* (2012, Innovation Press).

[15] 2006 film 'The Prestige' directed by Christopher Nolan, which was based on the 1995 book of the same name by British writer Christopher Priest, published by Touchstone.

[16] Situation – Complication – Solution is a shortened version of the SCQA (Situation – Complication – Question - Answer) approach to framing a solution – see Barbara Minto, *The pyramid principle: logic in writing and thinking* (3rd edn, 2008, Financial Times/Prentice Hall).

[17] This sentiment is presented in Zig Ziglar's book, *Staying up, up, up, in a down, down world* (2000, Thomas Nelson), as well as being part of his presentations and speeches.

4

SKILLS IN CHALLENGING THE CLIENT

This chapter brings together the skills that a consultant may draw on in order to add value by being appropriately challenging.

- *Section 1* looks at the 'zones of debate' and especially the 'Zone of Uncomfortable Debate'.
- *Section 2* discusses the 'hilltops' metaphor and the importance of recognising differences in perspective in consulting work.
- *Section 3* discusses cognitive distance and how this can help provide challenge or aid the transference of knowledge between consultant and client.
- *Section 4* outlines the 'push-pull' approach to influence, with this section providing the introduction to six mechanisms for influence: 'listening'; 'questioning'; 'summarising'; 're-framing', 'advising'; 'going ahead and doing it anyway'.
- *Section 5* explores unconscious mental processes and influence.
- *Section 6* looks at individual client characteristics through the lens of the Social Styles Inventory.

1 The ZOUD and challenging the client

Professor Cliff Bowman promoted the idea of the ZOUD, or 'Zone of Uncomfortable Debate'.[1] The ZOUD is one of three levels of dialogue – or zones of debate – suggested by Bowman, and perhaps the one most relevant to challenging a client's thinking.

Figure 4.1: Zones of debate

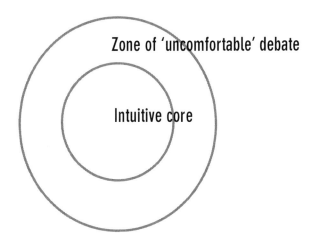

Zone of 'comfortable' debate

Zone of 'uncomfortable' debate

Intuitive core

The three zones of debate are the Zone of Comfortable Debate, the Zone of Uncomfortable Debate, and the Intuitive Core. All have a role in a consulting process, but the ZOUD is potentially the most productive and also the one many consultants find the most difficult.

The Zone of Comfortable Debate describes convivial conversation. What is being discussed between consultant and client is non-contentious. This means either that the subject is light and/or that both parties are in agreement. Dialogue in the Zone of Comfortable Debate will move a conversation forward, but usually in only two ways. It can provide a platform for reflection, helping the client's own thoughts to move their perspective on a situation. It can also work in a summarising capacity, where mutual acceptance of an opinion enables a conversation to progress to the next stage. However, it is in a social cohesion role that the Zone of Comfortable Debate makes its biggest contribution to effective dialogue. A challenging conversation can only really work if there is sufficient cohesion between the two parties. Cohesion keeps things together and mitigates against the tension that challenge causes. In many cultures an amount of comfortable debate is a necessary prequel to a conversation. The UK, for example draws heavily on the weather and the journey as a safe ground for this. One of our clients, who moved from an urban area to rural Shropshire on the English and Welsh border, spoke about what he referred to as "Shropshire sniffing time" which, in his experience, was a substantial chunk of time spent at the beginning of a conversation spent talking about not a great deal in particular prior to the real conversation being entered into. As an incomer, he'd learned to respect the sniffing time rather than seek to impose his greater sense of urgency.

The intuitive core of a conversation relates to the assumptions that both parties hold. Dialogue is more straightforward if assumptions are shared and often awkward if they are not.

In 2010 I was invited to be mentor to the Director of Strategy of a major UK enterprise. Prior to going along to meet the individual concerned, I researched what I thought was enough about the business to enable me to have a meaningful first meeting. The picture I built was of a prominent and successful commercial enterprise, big but privately owned, and active in a range of established and new technology sectors. My meeting progressed well but not swimmingly to start with. Those of you with experience of mentoring will understand that the relationship between mentor and mentee is a critical one, and obstructions here are detrimental to the value that a mentor may bring. The moment of realisation for me was when I learned that the enterprise's private ownership comprised over three hundred individual shareholders, all of whom were members of the same family. No shares were held (or to be held) outside of the family. My assumption that the business was focused on value creation to enable returns to investors was incorrect. The driver behind this business was one of continuity and legacy, the 'investors' weren't really able to trade their ownership, and the commercial focus was about being able to provide for the family over the longer term. One's approach to strategy is very different if this is the case.

The solution in respect of the intuitive core is an obvious one. Check out the assumptions. Many consultants develop their own way of raising questions about assumptions without giving the impression to their clients that they are either ill-prepared or lacking in intelligence. Shared understanding, a common intuitive core, enables a conversation to have pace and apply its energy to the main agenda.

The Zone of Uncomfortable Debate (ZOUD) is where challenging the client is most likely to happen. We will look in more detail at approaches and skills a consultant might use to achieve this. However, independent of the approach the consultant chooses to take is the recognition that the degree of discomfort in a conversation is not necessarily shared by both parties. On occasion, it may be the consultant who is feeling the discomfort while the client is totally prepared to be discomforted. I remember presenting the results of an organisational review to the senior management team of a client organisation, only to be told after my presentation that I had done an excellent job in pulling together the views of all the people in the organisation that I had interviewed or ran focus groups with, but what was my own opinion? My opinion was something that I had formed, but was not intending to disclose, until that moment. Conversely, experienced consultants have often flexed their muscles on how to be challenging, and for them it is second nature.

2 Hilltops

The diagram below illustrates the hilltops metaphor.[2] This actual diagram was created over 20 years ago, and we have used it with a range of clients to help illustrate the potential communication challenges between two people. The message behind hilltops is that two people may be looking at the same thing but they see differently because their vantage points are different. In our consulting skills context, on one hilltop is the consultant and on the other is the client. Both are looking at the same data (the spreadsheet, the slide deck), but because the perspective of each party is different, they each make distinct inferences. Many cultures have a way of expressing the same phenomenon, the point being that shortcomings in understanding perspectives often lead to problems in communication.

Figure 4.2: Hilltops

3 Social styles

This section looks at the application of personality profiling to the consulting context. Psychometric profiling will be familiar territory for many consultants and clients. Its potential value will be appreciated alongside its vulnerabilities (for example: single data point; the honesty of self-reflection; putting people into boxes; limits to its predictability of behaviour, and so on). The Social Styles Inventory is based on the Carl Jung psychology that underpins many psychometric tests, but is a 'lite' application. Its main quality, as a 'lite' approach, is that it is easy to use in the field. It does not need questionnaires and trained psychologists to apply. With sufficient emotional intelligence, an understanding of social styles can help a consultant connect more ably with a client, to the benefit of the project they are working on.[3]

The social styles approach encourages consultants to be sensitive to two factors: the degree to which the client is assertive, and the degree to which the client demonstrates emotional control. These are different constructs and, when related to each other, create a four-box grid with a different persona in each of the four areas. These four personas are usually labelled 'driver', 'expressive', 'analyser' and 'amiable'.

Figure 4.3: Social styles framework

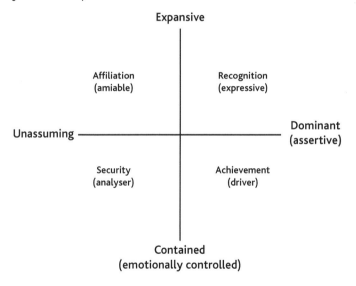

People who have high emotional control tend to be influenced by facts and specific data, whereas people who have less emotional control, and are more demonstrative with their feelings, tend to value personal relationships and interaction.

People who are more assertive tend to be bolder in their decision making, taking larger steps forward more readily. People who are less assertive will still make a decision, but will usually do so with smaller steps, often more tentatively. The Social Styles Inventory doesn't imply superior and inferior positions (there is no 'best place' for a person to be on the grid), it draws attention to the differences in natural style. A consultant is likely to be more effective when he or she can present information in a way that accords with the client's natural style.

Driver: high assertiveness / high emotional control – 'it's about achievement'

- A 'driver' makes decisions independently, with calculated risks and pretty much objectively.
- A consultant dealing with a driver is pacy and direct, keeps conversation on objectives and facts, and is not afraid to challenge the driver. The conversation is likely to be 'big picture' rather than 'detail'. Drivers don't like their time being wasted or having to engage in needless small talk.

Expressive: high assertiveness / low emotional control – 'it's about recognition'

- An 'expressive' makes decisions boldly, but with the involvement of others, and usually quickly.
- A consultant dealing with an expressive usually finds work matters are interlaced with a social element. Boundaries between work and play are blurred. Expressives are often charismatic, engaging leaders and enjoy being centre stage. Expressives do not like not holding a prominent role in what is going on.

Analyser: low assertiveness / high emotional control – 'it's about security'

- An 'analyser' makes decisions logically, carefully and often reluctantly.
- A consultant working with an analyser will become accustomed to a more deliberate decision-making process, a slower pace, and

needing to sate the analyser's appetite for detail and tendency towards procrastination due to uncertainty. Analysers don't like to have bullshit fed to them: it's a mark of strength for a consultant to say to an analyser "I don't know", instead making an off-the-cuff guestimate.

Amiable: low assertiveness / low emotional control – 'it's about affiliation'

- An 'amiable' makes decisions usually in terms of people, with the involvement of others and reluctantly.
- A consultant dealing with an amiable will understand the amiable's concern for the impact of their decision on other people, and will become used to the gentler approach that is helpful in encouraging a decision. Amiables treat the relationship with the consultant as an important part of the decision-making process. Betrayals of trust hit amiables hard, as does pressure to make a decision.

Where to start? – a consultant won't need to spend much time in the company of a client to develop a feel for the approach to use to connect with the client. If in doubt, experience suggests that a safe place for a consultant to operate initially is slightly in the 'driver' space. The combination of keeping conversation business-like, rather than social, with an element of energy brought to a conversation, is usually a safe starting point.

What about 'authenticity'? – as in leadership, one of the most prized qualities in consulting is authenticity.[4] This is the ability of the consultant to be himself or herself in the way they conduct themselves, and not put on an act. Often clients have an innate sense of whether a consultant is being genuine or not and, for the most part, people are unconvincing actors. Questions are sometimes asked about how a consultant can be authentic at the same time as modifying their style and approach in response to different client contexts. The answer is straightforward. Authenticity is about principles, ethics and values that sit at the core of a consultant's practice. When a consultant has clarity around these factors, principles, ethics and values should drive whatever a consultant does and wherever they do it. It is understandable if a consultant adopts a different style in dealing with the chief executive of a national funding body compared to dealing with frontline workers in a local care charity. Adapting style need not be disingenuous, but blowing with the breeze of ethics and values is. The stakeholder map in the social research arena is a particularly complex one, and consultants who thrive in this setting typically have well-developed skills in working with a wide range of people. Consistency around values and ethics is the bedrock of trust. Having the emotional intelligence to adopt approaches that are most helpful to the client's project is the practice skill that is built on that bedrock.

4 Cognitive distance

Cognitive distance is about the degree to which the demeanour and appearance of the consultant are similar to or different from the client.[5] The term has its roots in cognitive behavioural therapy: a person with high cognitive distance has the ability to disconnect full emotional identification from another party, and be significantly different. The converse applies. Someone with low cognitive distance connects naturally with the other party. They beat to the rhythm of the same drum.

The understanding of cognitive distance in consulting is valuable, as certain types of work favour low cognitive distance, where the consultant is 'like' the client, whereas other projects benefit from a substantial separation of perspective between consultant and client.

Social researchers will be familiar with using interviewers who are similar in demeanour and appearance to those being interviewed. This has the benefit of helping interviewees feel less daunted, wary or overawed. Some years ago, when my firm had a consulting project to carry out an evaluation of a prominent jazz music festival, we used an interviewer team who looked just as likely to be at home at a concert of world-class jazz as those people who had bought tickets to attend.

The interviewers were selected on the basis of their low cognitive distance from those who they were interviewing. Come the interval, the concertgoers were happy enough to spend a few minutes answering our interviewers' questions over their gin and tonics. In the same year, we used a different interviewer team to conduct the fieldwork on a pilot of Glasgow's weekend night bus service. Low cognitive distance was still useful, but the clientele were very different to those at the jazz festival, so the interview team we used had different characteristics.

Where the consultant has to form a strong connection with the client, in order to gather information or transfer knowledge, low cognitive distance is useful. Consultants who, for example, work in the operations management arena often think, look and act like their operations manager clients – being 'on the same wavelength' as the client, ideas and expertise flow readily from the consultant and find fertile ground. The danger of too low a cognitive distance will be recognised by many clients, and there is the risk of the consultant doing what is known in the sector as 'going native'. Here the consultant becomes so drawn into the client's context that she or he loses the objectivity which is part of their stock in trade. Long-term projects with high assignment intimacy (a lot of time on site in the company of the client team) are particularly vulnerable, as are projects which have an after-hours / social dimension to them.

High cognitive distance between consultant and client is useful in contexts where part of the consultant's *raison d'être* is the fact that they are selling a capability from a very different world to that inhabited by the client. A few years ago, my firm needed to upgrade its online learning platform, online learning support being part of our commercial portfolio. Our platform's capability had been eclipsed by advances in software, and its shortcomings made even more evident by the progressively higher expectations of users. During the course of scanning the market for a specialist supplier, I was encouraged on meeting Nick. Nick was casually dressed, though not in a smart way, extensively tattooed and half my age. When the small talk in our first meeting moved to Barcelona, from where Nick had just returned, he ventured that he wasn't too sure what the weather was like as he was asleep during the day. Here was someone so unlike me that it reinforced my hope that he was able to do things that I could not. The vulnerability of high cognitive distance is that the gulf between client and consultant is so great that it becomes very difficult for the consultant to impart expertise. She or he suffers from what is referred to as the burden of 'otherness'. At the extreme, people with a high cognitive distance are sometimes referred to as 'being on a different planet'.

There is no single best place for a consultant to be in respect of cognitive distance. There should, however, be an appreciation of the impact that perceived (by the client) cognitive distance may have on the ability to connect with or add value to a client through being different.

For people working in an internal consulting role, cognitive distance is a harder construct to manage, and is contextually less malleable. As a consequence of working in the same organisation as the client, the consultant's persona and demeanour is pretty much anchored. She or he may wish to draw on the benefits of cognitive distance to help communicate ideas or to be challenging to the internal client, but the consultant's existing organisational visibility and backstory more or less mean little freedom of movement in this regard for the consultant. But what the internal consultant loses, in respect of managing cognitive distance, he or she gains on the contextual understanding and their political grasp (politics being the art of the possible) of the landscape in which the consulting work will take place.

5 Push pull influencing

A central function of consulting interventions is to bring something original to the client: a challenge to what would otherwise have happened, if you will. The push-pull model of influence contributes to our understanding of challenge by illustrating some of the main mechanisms by which a client can be challenged, and presenting them in a framework whereby the relationship between them can be more deeply appreciated.[6]

Figure 4.4: Push-pull influencing

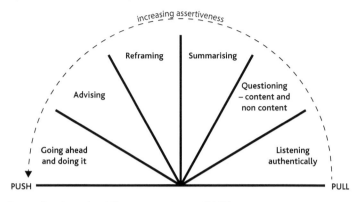

Source: Developed from Wickham and Wickham (2008)

The main dynamic in the arrangement of the activities is the degree of assertiveness which each of the approaches is based on. The assumption in the model is that all are well-intentioned and executed responsibly.

Where to start – despite many explanations of consulting based around the process of giving advice, the core skill is that of listening. Below, we will look at how the process of listening to the client enables challenge. The subsequent trajectory around the model is from right to left – listening being followed by questioning, then summarising and, as the assertiveness rises, into reframing, advising and then going ahead with action.

The capable consultant has two attributes in relation to the push-pull model. First, they are confident and capable in all the six elements. Second, they have the ability to know which to use and when. Their skills are well beyond that of a one-trick pony, and their dexterity with the mechanisms means that they do not bump into the furniture when working with the client.

The dark underbelly – the shadow side of the push-pull model relates to the misdirected use of the mechanisms. When the focus moves away from the responsible use of the approach for the benefit of the client, problems arise. These influencing techniques are powerful, so this is as much an issue of professionalism or ethics as anything else. Examples of the misuse of the model include selective listening followed by selective summarising, where what is summarised is true but incomplete. They also include questioning for self-gain, reframing to amplify client insecurity (for example, "what is the rest of the organisation going to think if you don't move ahead with the next phase of the work, having made this commitment to everyone four months ago?"), advice without the necessary foundation, and taking action that sets in motion a path dependency of actions which is hard to stop.

The following looks at each of the six elements of the push-pull model in turn, starting with probably the core skill for many consultants: listening.

5.1 Listening

It is hard to argue against the merits of good listening skills as a key component of the consultant's skillset. The push-pull perspective frames listening beyond the ability to gather information and learn things from discussions, and sees it in the context of being able to challenge a client.

Before looking at how being listened to can provide a challenge to a client's perspective, it is useful to recap the foundations of effective listening. The idea of levels of listening[7] draws attention to the importance of the listener being 'in the room', and to listening being empathic and based on the other party's frame of reference and not the consultant's own. In this mode the listener is connected to what is being said and engaged in the conversation. This will be evident in the listener's feeling for the conversation and the way his or her body language comes across to the listener.

A word about mirroring – in the context of a face-to-face interaction between two people, mirroring means one party deliberately managing their body language to bring it into step with that of the other party. The gravity behind the idea is the understanding that the majority of communication between two people is non-verbal. Even when words are being spoken, and tone and pitch of voice are modulated accordingly to help emphasise meaning, non-verbal signals communicate the bulk of the information. The science behind mirroring is the recognition that when, in this case, two people are relating to each other really well, their body language falls into step with each other: it mirrors. This is readily observed when looking at good friends in a social situation and often, if one person alters their posture or body language, the other follows suit. These are unconscious actions: people generally do not know they are doing it.

The twist happened when mirroring became coached and people were encouraged to develop the skill of reading the body language of another party and deliberately bring their own into alignment. This is about ingratiation by sending signals of positive engagement to be unconsciously interpreted by the other party. There is little doubt that this is potentially powerful, and it is widely used in sales training, for example. The two issues that temper my enthusiasm for it, as a valuable skill for consultants, are ethics and practicality. The ethical standpoint is perhaps obvious. The only legitimate reason for a consultant to use techniques of influence and manipulation is if it improves their ability to act in the best interests of the client. The practicality issue is about the, in my experience, limited ability of people in general to be good at mirroring.

In 2011, I was working as part of a team at Durham University Business School, with a client who was one of the UK's main retail banks. The backdrop to the project was that the recession the previous year had rendered many businesses financially precarious, and many business bankers nervous. The scenario was one of the business being in debt to the bank and not being in a position meet its financial obligations. Our role was to help the business bank team prepare for difficult conversations with such business clients. In one of the development exercises, the bank manager was paired with a client (we used professional actors to roleplay the clients). The bank manager was briefed to initiate the face-to-face conversation with the client and do nothing more than listen in a fully engaged manner to what the client had to say. The duration of this task was three minutes. The value of the task is explained below when we return to how listening can challenge a client's thinking. However, on one occasion a bank manager and actor were staged in front of the other 15 people in the group, and the conversation was started by the banker. What happened over the next three minutes was on the verge of appearing comical to the observers. The actor played his part straight and, while he recognised what was going on, did nothing to egg his interviewer on. When the actor changed his posture, the bank manager responded. Whether this was the crossing of legs, the canting of head, or the shifting of weight from one side to the other, the banker mirrored the actions of the other party. After three minutes, we unpacked (debriefed) the task and sought feedback from all present. The primary observation was how obvious the attempts at mirroring were to everyone else. It totally missed the mark of connecting on a subconscious level. It's probably fair to say that, unless you are a skilled actor, leave attempts to mirror well alone because very few people have the skill to do it well. I asked the bank manager concerned about what he remembered of what his client had told him over those three minutes. The bank manager's answer endorsed the second reason why mirroring is an overrated aspiration for many. Whereas the banker was able to remember some of what he was told, by his own admission his grasp was too light to be of use in a real conversation, because he was concentrating so much on the body language.

Moving towards empathic listening – some sagely guidance that came my way from a very experienced consultant was to let the body language look after itself. Focus on the client and what the client is saying, and if you are, to use the expressions from earlier, 'in the room' and 'feeling' the conversation, your body will respond accordingly.

There is one safety check I would recommend when following the above guidance. This is about the use of the 'third eye'. Once I was working with teams of business advisors preparing them to have better consulting conversations with clients. One of the tasks in the skills development workshop involved a 25-minute interview with a client by a panel of three business advisors. As with the above example, I had engaged professional actors to take the role of the client, and I sat at one of the flanks of the interview room as an observer. The three people in the business advisor team organised themselves, with one taking the lead on the questions, another taking notes, and the third person poised to ask additional questions as necessary. After the interview was finished the five of us in the room reflected on how the task had gone. As I thought would happen, the actor gave the most powerful feedback to the third business advisor, who had said very little in the interview and concentrated fully on what the client was saying. The actor proceeded to tell him that he found his body language oppressive, to the point that it was offputting, certainly not conducive to the rapport that would have been helpful to productive dialogue. The business advisor was experienced, took the task seriously, and was perturbed that his genuine attempt at empathetic listening had faltered. I asked the actor how he managed his body language when he was on stage or in front of a TV camera. He said he imagined he had a third eye which looked down on him from about one metre away and could let him know how he was appearing to others (he extended his arm to a space in front of him, slightly above his head to show its location). "Every now and then" said the actor, "I check in with my third eye".

This angle on the management of body language takes the emphasis away from mirroring and places it strongly on empathic listening, with the occasional health check through the third eye.

Professional coach Nancy Kline helps us to appreciate that listening to a client helps the client to challenge his or her thinking. In Nancy's experience a client is capable of resolving their own issues and arriving at their own solutions 70% of the time, without the need for anything other than the opportunity to be listened to.[8] The client, after all, is the world's foremost expert on their own situation. The problem is that the opportunity to have the attention of a skilled listener is rare.

Our brains work far more quickly than we are able to speak. We can have thoughts in various different directions in the time it takes us to say a sentence. We can only say one thing at once, which means that to speak we have to put our thoughts in some kind of order. The process of articulation also raises our thoughts to our consciousness (which is why we should proofread by reading out loud rather than reading silently). Many will be familiar with the expression to 'talk a problem through', which is a tacit endorsement of the approach. Our skill is to create the environment for our clients to be comfortable with talking and developing their own stream of consciousness in real time. For this to work, it needs not only the management of the physical environment in which the conversation is to take place, but also empathic listening of the highest order.

It is perhaps worth reflecting that people often think they are better listeners than they are in reality. In one study, general practitioners were asked how much time they gave their patients to explain their symptoms before they intervened with questions or comments.[9] The results of the study showed that general practitioners' estimates of how much listening they did were far in excess of the actual amount. Nancy Kline's encouragement is to "pay beautiful attention" to the client and "don't even think about interrupting". Nancy is able to initiate a conversation with a phrase like "what would you like to talk about today?", which is open and non-directive, allowing the client to bring to the table whatever issue they wish, and then have a 'conversation' with the client for around half an hour, saying nothing save the occasional non-directive encouragement, such as "and what else?") as appropriate. She will use her own silence to allow the client to gather their thoughts and to encourage the client to continue talking and fill the void (Nancy's silence is more of a safe space of anticipation than an awkward pause). She is unlikely to ask detailed questions or offer advice, and she has the ability to sense when her client has come to the end of what they wanted to cover. At no time will Nancy's demeanour give the merest impression that she wants to interrupt.

There is a well-tested approach to helping clients flex their muscles in this skill area that I learned from mentoring specialist Professor David Megginson. It needs groups of three, one to be the client, one to be the consultant (and listen in the style of Nancy Kline), and one to observe. The client brings to the table any subject they choose, providing it is both real and unresolved. Real means a genuine issue (we are largely incapable of creating fiction in sufficient detail to be convincing, on the hoof). Unresolved means the client is not replaying something that has already been resolved. These two conditions accepted, the choice of the subject is totally open. It doesn't have to be profound or earth-shattering. During my work with consultants on skills development workshops, "where should we go on our next holiday?", "which school should we send the twins to?", "should I buy a new bicycle?", "which parents-in-law should we spend Christmas day with?", "should my partner return to work?", are examples that various people have worked with. The listening task runs for around three minutes, after which the observer leads on the feedback.

The more skilled listeners have enabled clients to move their thinking forward and, by their clients' own admission, make connections that had thus far missed them, and consider implications that had otherwise escaped them. Similarly, the better listeners have often been surprised by what the clients have said towards the end of the three minutes – insights that would have probably remained buried had the consultant shifted their approach to questioning or giving advice.

If the above task attracts criticism it is in these two ways. Sometimes people in the consultant role say it is unnatural to be in a conversation for three minutes and not say anything. Sometimes those in the client role said they wanted some form of input from the consultant during the three minutes, for example a question or some feedback, to help move the conversation on. The skill being developed here, though, is not about developing three-minute listening skills, it is about learning to be a better listener. In the field, the consultant will sense when might be the right time to ask a question or pull together a summary, but if a consultant who can listen ably for 30 seconds can do the same for a minute, he or she might create the conditions for the client to make their transition in thinking, or for them as consultants to learn something they otherwise would not.

Listening and taking notes – we have touched on the subject of note-taking earlier in this book. The issue here is the detrimental effect note-taking has on eye contact. Note-taking in conversations has two main plus points. It shows reverence for what is being said, and it enables the capturing of detail that otherwise might be beyond the recall powers of the consultant. In many cultures, good eye contact is an essential ingredient of productive dialogue. The most useful guidance

I had regarding taking effective notes without losing the connection with the client through insufficient eye contact, came from Dr Andy Lowe, one of my academic supervisors. Andy's advice was, with permission, to take keyword notes during the interview. In this way the bulk of the attention can be devoted to the client and not to the notepad. After the interview is finished and the consultant and client have gone their separate ways, the consultant should go back over the notes and augment the keywords with other relevant information. The keywords act as a prompt on the recall. The discipline necessary for this to work is for the consultant to do this within half a day of the interview, when the memory is fresh. Discussions with empathic listening are high-tariff work that are often draining of energy if done well, and after the conclusion of such a discussion, usually the last thing the consultant feels like doing is going back over the notes. But if this task is left, to be returned to at a later date, the consultant's recall is likely to be sparse. The term 'discipline', which appears above, was a deliberate inclusion – normally the last thing a consultant wants to do straight after a long interview, where they have been fully focused on the client, is to write up the notes.

5.2 Questioning

Following listening, the next mechanism in the push-pull model is questioning. Often a discussion, especially in the early stages, involves the interplay between questioning and listening. Rather than being a casual affair, the consultant realises the power of questions to not only challenge the client at that moment in time, but also to guide the conversation along particular lines of enquiry.

In skills development workshops with consultants, business advisers and mentors, I ask a volunteer to speak for about a paragraph (typically 30 seconds) on a challenge he or she faces that is unresolved. I then ask everyone else to write down the question they would most like to ask the volunteer (writing down means the exact words, from the initial capital letter to the final question mark). We then compare and reflect on the question, recognising that everybody in the room was given the same data to work with by the volunteer. The questions vary according to which path of investigation each person wished to follow. Some are exploratory while other questions seek confirmation. Some questions are non-directive while others home in on a particular issue. The overriding recognition is that the person asking the questions controls the conversation. It is easier for the person asking the questions to guide the conversation than it is for the one answering.

Questioning skills are typically part of the core armoury in social research. Below are four of the considerations around questioning that relate to the role of the consultant and the ability to challenge a client's thinking.

Purpose – fans of crime writing will have appreciated that a lawyer in a courtroom will ask a question to which he or she already knows the answer. The reason why relates to the purpose of the question. Sometimes we ask a question because we want to find out something we don't know; we may also ask a question because we would like the other party to think about it and, in the case of the courtroom, at other times we ask questions because we would like the resultant information to be shared with others, using a voice that is not our own. The point here is that, in a consulting role, we recognise the use of questions for objectives other than to find out information. In terms of challenging a client's thinking, questioning with the purpose of encouraging a client to think about a situation or issue can be particularly powerful.

Question style – social researchers usually have well-developed questioning skills. This includes funnelling –starting broad and then narrowing – moving from non-directive to directive questions and open questions to closed questions. 'Helicopter' questioning (to raise or lower the focus of the conversation) can be applied to probing. The majority of open questions in the English language start with the word 'what'. Using 'what' keeps the focus of the conversation at the same level, which makes for a more nimble conversation with flow. Starting a question with the word 'how' drops the focus into the detail. 'How' questions are particularly useful if a client is being too vague or abstract. 'Why' questions, on the other hand, raise the focus of the discussion into motives and rationale. Ideally, 'why' questions are used sparingly, as they are comparatively harder to answer than other forms. When a 'why' question is focused on the client as the subject, for example, "why did you…?", this combination is particularly intrusive.

Facts are our friends – there is great value to specific answers to questions in a consulting context, even accepting that specific answers may be nothing more than unfounded perceptions. Words offered by clients like 'fine', increase', 'strong', 'leading', 'robust' convey sentiment, but that is about all. They are too vague as answers for the consultant to interpret with a high degree of confidence. For example, does 'leading' mean number one in the market by scale, or the brand with the highest brand equity, or does it imply thought leadership and trend setting? All are legitimate interpretations. As answers to a consultant's questions, vague sentiments can be useful as part of a conversation, but are usually best served by a follow-up question to ask the client what he or she meant. Firm and specific data is more useful as a foundation for subsequent work. On many occasions I have worked with senior leaders in a client organisation and been able to surface perceptual differences in each of their thinking by deliberately probing initial answers with factual questions. The devil is in the detail. Many consulting projects involve the surfacing of perceptual differences and the subsequent facilitation towards an aligned understanding (for example, in helping a team to agree the targets and goals for a road safety initiative).

Prefixing – a prefix in front of a question helps the interviewee to contextualise what is being asked. In the pursuit of motive, precision and understanding, consultants can come across as nosey and pushy. The prefix means that the sentence does not start with the question, but provides a few words of warm-up and the opportunity for the person being interviewed to get his or her head around the subject. The technique was shared with me by mentoring specialist Professor David Megginson. David was working with one of the UK's police forces, training senior officers to be mentors for junior officers. Police officers undergo substantial training in questioning technique, but the focus is investigative, with a power differential between the person asking the questions and the one answering. It is not structured as a conversation between equals: the interviewee is expected to be totally disclosive, while the police officer will give little away. That power differential might work well for interrogating suspects, but it can be offputting in a development setting where the discussion between consultant and client is better served by being more equally balanced. Prefixing questions was one of the most useful techniques that David introduced the officers to, as a means to more conversational questioning, for example "to help me build a picture of what happened about the funding, why did the meeting approve the budget for that project?". The prefix gives the opportunity for the client to understand the motive behind the question, which has the impact of taking some of the perceived threat and challenge out of the question. As a result, the conversation between client and consultant should flow more readily.

5.3 Summarising

Mentoring expert, Professor Bob Garvey,[10] believes that the ability to summarise is the most powerful single contributor towards an effective negotiation. It is easy to appreciate his point, and summarising skills should be part of any consultant's toolkit.

The power behind summarising is threefold. First, in order to summarise the consultant has to listen to what is being said. What better way to show respect for a person than to have listened to them and be able to demonstrate that you remember? The demonstration of listening is made even more powerful in that summaries are more condensed than the data upon which they are based, so they veer more towards sharpness than verbosity. In presenting the understanding in his or her own words, the consultant demonstrates not only the ability to listen and remember, but also the more valuable skill of being able to listen and understand. Often a consultant will rephrase the client's words as a means of demonstrating an interest in and grasp of a situation. Second, the summary works as a means of checking understanding. Periodic summarising through the course of a conversation enables the evolution of understanding to stay on track (if understanding drifts it can be readily corrected), and this trail of consciousness becomes the foundation of co-created and/or further insight. Third, the ability to summarise well (meaning the client is likely to agree with the summary) brings consultant and client together on the one 'hilltop'. No matter how difficult or challenging the conversation has been, the sharing of a vantage point (even if for a brief period of time) brings consultant and client side by side, with the benefit of an agreed perspective. Viewing things in the same way as the client enables the consultant to use this shared understanding as a platform to further develop the conversation.

The content to summarise comes from the consultant listening and questioning. Summarising should be an iteration with listening and questioning, and provide a periodic catching of breath in a discussion that pulls together both the data and the parties in the conversation. The role of summarising in challenging a client's thinking can often be amplified by this one twist: ask the client to articulate the summary. The act of saying it rather than just thinking it brings to the conscious mind that which might have otherwise lacked that gravity. Giving that responsibility to the client can help to unlock ideas in the client's mind that the consultant's summary might have been unable to do.

5.4 Reframing

As we move around the push-pull influencing model and the means of challenging the client's thinking becomes more assertive, the step beyond summarising is reframing. In reframing, the client is figuratively lifted from his or her hilltop and put on someone else's. Reframing is particularly useful if a client is unable to view an issue in the round. If the blinkers are on, to ask them to consider the same issue from another angle can sometimes be what is required. "I hear what you say about the need to restructure, but could you just see this from your team's perspective?".

5.5 Advising and recommending

Providing advice sits centrally in many people's understanding of what a consultant does – we made that point in the first section of the first chapter. As a way of helping to challenge a client's thinking, advice giving in its direct form carries with it a high degree of assertion. With that, it carries the potential risk of alienating the client, if it is not handled with finesse. Here are some phrases I have noted that are used by different consultants in their face-to-face discussions with clients:

> Why don't you go with your instinct and… ?
> To play devil's advocate for a minute, have you considered… ?
> The prevailing message from the data appears to be…
> There's a lot of support for xxx course of action, out there.
> Another client faced this challenge, what worked for them is…
> If you were to do this, I think you'd generate…
> I'll say what my recommendation is, and also why.
> If I was in your shoes, I would…

There are two themes in the examples which might help as a guide towards more effective advice giving. These themes are about how the advice is evidenced and the style with which the advice is presented.

- *Muster the evidence* – the phrase 'shoot the messenger' points out the danger of placing oneself in the line of fire, especially in situations where sound relationships are key. One of the themes in the above is that many of the phrases reach out for justification, such that the voice for change is not that of the consultant. Rather than being the messenger, the consultant is the signposter. This not only takes the consultant out of the line of fire, but also potentially adds some heft to the guidance being proffered and enables the consultant, like the client, to stand to one side of the data and look at the situation with increased objectivity. Lurking in the shadow side of all of this is the understanding that there is so much data, a consultant has the scope to pretty much pick and choose the data that suits his or her purpose. If they cannot lay their hands on a viewpoint that reinforces their view, the consultant can just make it up. The phrase 'devil's advocate' legitimises anything being brought into the conversation, irrespective of provenance.

- *Choose the style* – one of the other patterns in the examples is the range of styles each of the consultants has used to present their arguments, the choice of style being driven by the type of client rather than the type of consultant. We see the presentation to a numerate, analytically-thinking client ("the prevailing message in the data seems to be…"), and also to the client who is more of a people person ("there's a lot of support for…"). There is presentation to the more confident client ("why don't you just go with your instinct?") and to the client who may need more reassurance ("another client who faced a similar problem…"). We look further into the importance of style difference when we look at Social Styles later in this chapter.

- *Giving it straight* – on occasion, the consultant has little option but to present advice straight and unfettered. The advantage is that the client is probably left in no doubt as to what your opinion is, which can be a major plus if you have been commissioned as an expert consultant. But there is no finesse or sense of self-discovery for the client here. Sometimes the view held by the consultant is at odds with the view the client may hold. In this form, advice giving is direct but it is also confrontational. The consultant is the messenger and realises they will probably be shot in the process.

There is an example concerning Marvin Bower in this respect. Marvin was a very experienced management consultant who was the architect of the rise in prominence of McKinsey and Company. On one occasion, he had tried various less assertive approaches to help the client's enlightenment, but none of these worked. He knew he would be delinquent in his duty if did anything other than give his opinion, in the full knowledge that was likely to be toxic to the relationship.

Marvin did not shirk his responsibility to be valuable to the client and told Mr Little, the Chief Executive Officer of the client organisation that "the problem, Mr Little, is you".[11]

For the vast majority of the push-pull model, the consultant can possibly enjoy that dual quality of being both respected and liked. But with confrontational advice giving, that relational axis may suffer. The tension is that people are more readily influenced by people they like, and to be respected is the foundation of personal reputation – which is probably the most valuable commodity a consultant is likely to possess. If in doubt, sacrifice being liked in favour of the courage of your convictions and the sense of integrity that comes from this. It is unlikely that this will be a pleasant process (one of my consulting colleagues refers to such encounters as 'meetings without coffee'), especially in the short term, but today's reputation is tomorrow's money.

There is an encouraging twist in the Marvin Bower story. In corporate America, the typical tenure in years of a CEO can be counted on the digits of one hand. Within a few years Mr Little was no longer CEO, and when the new CEO came on board and set about hiring management consultants, the firm he chose was McKinsey. The reason was that he could trust them to be upfront and honest.

Armed with the knowledge that there is the possibility that some news you as a consultant will wish to impart to the client may be particularly challenging for the client to receive, it might be useful to frame this in the pre-contract discussions with the client, or at least at the commissioning meeting. Having such a conversation about the 'ground rules' of the relationship can ease possible tension if and when such a situation arises. If the conversation takes place at pre-contract stage, both consultant and client can form their opinions as to whether they are likely to have a fruitful relationship.

The former head of McKinsey's strategy practice, Kevin Coyne, talks about his own style as a consultant in an explanatory video he produced with his own strategy consulting practice.[12] "We come from the tell it like it is school", he says, "if I believe 'X', I will say 'X'". Coyne's standing in the industry is such that he can pretty much select the clients his firm wants to work with, and indeed the firm works with clients who are comfortable with this direct approach. There is an added advantage that comes from this forthrightness, and it is that the client trusts that the consultant has the mettle to keep the story consistent: "If I say 'X' here, you can trust me to keep saying 'X'".

5.6 Going ahead and doing it

The final part of the push-pull model, and the most extreme form of assertion in the concept, is where the consultant takes it upon himself or herself to effect change on behalf of the client. In some situations this can be the most, if not the only form of effective influence.

The basis of it is the behavioural heuristic which attracts people to the most convenient course of action. We gravitate towards that which is easy rather than that which is more difficult. In this form of influence, the consultant reduces the degree to which a step for a client is daunting, by taking action to make the step less of a big one, and reduce the amount of work the client needs to do. This can involve completing paperwork for the client, without the client having asked for this to be done. It could also be making a phone call to set a meeting up for a client, again without having the nod in advance, or having a pre-emptive discussion with a stakeholder prior to obtaining the client's permission.

It can be easy for the consultant to overstep the mark here, for the client to feel disempowered or even railroaded into a course of action; so the way the consultant frames influence of this nature is with both good intent and great care.

6 Unconscious mental processes and influence

The final section looks at automatic and unconscious neural processes, and their impact on how a client may process information and arrive at decisions. This school of thought falls within behavioural economics, and represents a more insightful view into decision-making behaviour than the previously held perspective that people are able to make rational decisions, do so on the basis of substantial information, and can mobilise their independent agency to act. This is moving the rational/ logical perspective of consulting (favoured, for example, by Barbara Minto with her pyramid principle) into a more holistic painting of the situation, where client systems are political and cognitive constructs. Rather than replacing the role of logic and rational thinking in consulting, these widen the consultant's repertoire of how to challenge the client in the pursuit of being valuable.

The impact of unconscious mental processes on human decision making has been getting greater attention over recent years. Daniel Kahneman popularised the distinction between thinking fast and thinking slow,[13] performance coach Steve Peters wrote about the chimp paradox,[14] while Jonathan Haidt used the metaphor of the elephant and the rider.[15] In these cases the former ('fast', the chimp and the elephant) represent the powerful, in the moment, instinctive component of human behaviour, in comparison with the rational and considered perspective.

When I am working with teams of managers and consultants on this issue, I often start the discussion by showing a slide with the following:

> … if you've ever slept in, said something in the heat of the moment that you later regretted, over-eaten, ordered the extra drink you didn't need, chosen the chocolate brownie over the fruit salad, tried to and failed to give up smoking, skipped the morning run or the evening gym session, abandoned your language class or piano lessons…

Most people identify with several of these, and on occasion with all of them! The cameos illustrate the power of the instinctive thinking fast, chimp-like/elephantine component of how people actually make decisions in their everyday lives, compared to how people like to believe they approach decision making, from a logical and rational perspective.

6.1 Decision-making biases

The study of cognitive biases and heuristics (a heuristic is a rule of thumb) has shed light on some of the deviations that people make from a path of rational decision making. This is not to trivialise the importance of logical thinking in the consulting world. To be able to present ideas and arguments in a logical and rational way is highly valuable, but it is also insufficient in many contexts. The consultant's armoury is strengthened by a practical grasp of how unconscious mental processes affect client decision making and the ability to either influence or be influenced.[16] There is a rational perspective to the way that consulting issues can be framed, but there are political and cognitive perspectives too.

- *Anchoring* describes the tendency to rely too heavily on the first piece of information offered (the anchor) when making decisions. That initial piece of data has a subconscious but profound effect on subsequent judgments. The initial quantifications of cost savings, first stabs at budgets for development projects, projections for the uptake of new services, are not just estimates. They become the unconsciously accepted expectation.[17]
- *Confirmation bias* is the characteristic that we are inclined to seek information that supports our beliefs, and are less inclined to be open to information that contradicts them. In the consulting context, confirmation bias can lead to both consultants and clients being selective in their consideration of data and information. People can draw on information that supports their own views, self-justifying their perspectives. People can also be closed-minded to opinions which are counter to theirs.
- *Over-confidence bias* is the characteristic whereby people place greater confidence in their estimating ability than is warranted. Making estimates is one of the necessary parts of consulting practice. Often consultants are working with incomplete data, face budget and/or time constraints, or are looking at future issues where no firm data exists. Consultants by and large are

happy to make estimates and understand their limitations, but the process by which estimates come about can muddy the waters. For a consultant to make an estimate, he or she has to build some form of equation or algorithm into which to drop the data. The data come with assumptions and the consultant will work to ensure that specific data points are based on reasonable assumptions. When the consultant is asked about the degree of confidence they have in their estimates, people typically reply with higher levels of confidence than is the reality. The reason for such over-confidence is that the scrutiny of the estimate is based on the same algorithm and assumptions as the estimate itself – meaning the scrutiny confirms the estimate and reinforces it. Making estimates will remain a part of consulting, and over-confidence bias warns consultants from being too wedded to the formula they create and the data assumptions they draw on.

- *Sunk cost fallacy* is a heuristic in client decision making which consultants are likely to experience across a range of client situations. In sunk cost fallacy, the disposition for a client to continue with an enterprise can be influenced by how much has already been invested. Prior commitment (sunk cost) can create a path dependency that is hard to alter in client projects. The term 'throw good money after bad' will be known to most, and it reminds us that previous investment is no guarantee of eventual success.

- *Risk aversion* goes beyond the fallacy of sunk costs and clouds the assessment of opportunity. Research finds that people have a greater disposition to gamble when faced with positions of potential loss, and a lower disposition to gamble when the context is one of potential gain. People are typically more concerned about potential loss than gain. This can lead to a situation where an organisation, which is currently performing strongly, is less likely to make speculative investments in future initiatives. An enterprise which is facing significant challenges in respect of its viability gets drawn into cavalier actions. The converse is more healthy – investments are better made from positions of strength, and the expression 'throw good money after bad' points out the general futility of desperate speculation.[18]

- *Hindsight bias* is the inclination to retrospectively see an event as predictable, despite the absence of an objective basis for predicting it at the time. In hindsight bias, people look back to create tidy explanations for the outcomes of complex situations – a desire driven by a natural aversion to ambiguity. Consultants encourage learning from experience in their own practice and that of their clients. While reflection is good, hindsight bias points out that it is easy to be reflective and see a false image in the mirror.[19]

There are other examples of bias and arational reasoning in the way that consultants and clients might process information and frame decisions.

- *Wilful blindness* is a wilful ignorance of the facts. It also known as Nelsonian knowledge, named after the naval commander Lord Nelson who raised his telescope to his blind eye and reported that he could see no ships. In wilful blindness there is the lack of ability to make the connections between the pieces of evidence. In some cases, as in Nelsonian knowledge, this can be a deliberate act. Often consultants will use terms like 'wake up and smell the coffee' when frustrated by their client's inability to join the dots and grasp the reality. In other situations it could be an unwillingness to face the facts for fear of the picture they might paint and the threat they imply. Consultants will sometimes refer to clients 'having their heads in the sand' in order protect themselves from what would otherwise be in front of them.[20]
- *Mere exposure* – we have in our nature a heuristic which psychologists refer to as 'mere exposure' – the old adage 'familiarity breeds contempt' is wrong. 'Familiarity breeds content' – people are more likely to find favour with concepts that are familiar to them, as distinct from new (this is why 'branding' is so important in competitive arenas). In terms of challenging a client's thinking, mere exposure emphasises the

value of socialising ideas beforehand, rather than introducing surprises at decision time, for example in the recommendations section of the final report.

- *Curse of knowledge* is a two-pronged characteristic which can affect consultants and clients alike. The first prong relates to the notion that it is difficult for someone who 'knows' something to appreciate that others find it difficult to understand how others cannot grasp it like they can. This can impact heavily on expert consultants who, when challenged by their client to slow down and go back over what they have just said, step by step, become slightly frustrated – which detracts from their ability to have the ear of their client. The second prong is more about the client situation when he or she is called upon to make a decision that the client already knows (as with mere familiarity) has unduly high gravity. Even though a consultant may wish a client to have an open mind when viewing data, when people are exposed to multiple and complex messages (as is increasingly the case in today's world), there is a tendency for people to drop back onto the certainty of what they already know. Once something is 'known' it is very difficult for that person to 'un-know' it.

6.2 Mental shortcuts and influence

The above examples show how our mental processes can temper the rational consideration of information – how heuristics or mental shortcuts drive choice and behaviour in ways that are not logical. This thread has been followed with research into how people can use mental shortcuts in the influencing of others. For a consultant, this serves as a reminder of the mechanisms, beyond rational arguments and logical explanation, by which clients make choices. Robert Cialdini's work has brought together some of the most useful 'autopilot' means to influence, of relevance to a consulting setting. Beyond persuading people through the use of logic, Cialdini suggests additional ways in which people are influenced to take action and prioritise their attention.[21]

- *Reciprocity* – people seek to repay those they owe. If a consultant does something the client considers valuable, it creates a credit in the bank of goodwill, which disposes the client towards the reciprocal action. For a consultant to avail themselves of reciprocity, he or she should have first made the investment to earn the credit.
- *Social proof* – clients are readily influenced by the actions of those they see as like themselves. Human beings are herd animals and are influenced by the behaviour of others in their herd. This is how and why market segmentation works, and also mimetic isomorphism in organisational change. For example, in a consulting context, a client may well be disposed to take the same action as someone in an equivalent role in a similar organisation, on the basis that the other party provided social proof of the soundness of that action.
- *Liking* – clients are more readily influenced by consultants they like. Consulting teams are potentially strong beneficiaries of this characteristic, as they present the client with more than one option for the creation of a strong and productive consultant-client relationship.
- *Authority* – clients can be more readily influenced by those with authority than by those without. The consultant might have expert power, but he or she might have authority resulting from senior-level sponsorship within a client organisation, or might have the authority inferred from the credentials on their CV (the act of a consultant enhancing their credentials and hence perceived authority is known as credentialising[22]).
- *Scarcity* – clients are disposed towards things they perceive as being in short supply. Being 'over-available' to a client is not always a healthy strategy for a consultant, while positioning opportunities as time-limited to clients usually is.

- *Instant influence* – clients typically favour that which gratifies immediately. 'Quick wins' or 'low-hanging fruit' work, and are often helpful in building enthusiasm for a consulting or change intiative.

From a slightly different angle, neuroscientist David Rock explored the potential stress raisers which conspire against effective influence.[23] Rock's research highlighted the dangers of diminishing someone's perceived status when encouraging them towards a particular course of action (a consultant knows the importance of making a primary client look good), and the value in presenting choice to clients such that they feel they have autonomy. Rock also emphasised the importance of certainty in influence. A strident consultant may boldly claim certainty of outcome as a means of mustering support, and use techniques like 'killer graphs' to present complex and ambiguous subjects as simple and certain. A killer graph will show two trajectories, often against a timeline, to draw attention to differences in direction of travel (for example, recommended strategy versus current strategy, our performance versus competitors' performance, scenario A versus scenario B).

This section has scratched the surface of the growing area of study into human decision making, and how so much of what we do happens without us consciously being aware of it. The power in some of these ideas presents the consultant with an ethical question to answer. These approaches can work just as well in situations that are destructive or selfish as they do in situations that are more wholesome and well-intentioned. How and when to use these techniques, as well as 'why', rests with the consultant, his or her conscience and the codes of ethics they subscribe to.

Notes

[1] See Cliff Bowman's 1995 paper, 'Strategy workshops and top team commitment to strategic change', *Journal of Managerial Psychology*, 10 (8).

[2] It is difficult to be precise about the origins of the 'hilltops' metaphor. The importance of seeing issues from the other party's perspective is well appreciated in different cultures around the world, for example the phrase 'don't judge a man until you've walked a mile in his shoes', which is often attributed to the Cherokee tribe of Native Americans.

[3] Social Styles theory is based on the work of David Merrill and Roger Reid, who used factor analysis to study two variables in people: assertiveness and emotional control (labelled responsiveness), while working in an insurance company in the 1960s, see *Personal styles and effective performance* (1999, New York: CRC Press).

[4] For example, the importance of a consultant being authentic is a key theme of Peter Block's landmark consulting book, *Flawless consulting: a guide to getting your expertise used* (3rd edn, 2011, Pfeiffer).

[5] Cognitive distance, as applied to consulting situations, see Andrew Sturdy, Karen Handley, Timothy Clark and Robin Fincham, *Management consultancy: boundaries and knowledge in action* (2010, Oxford University Press).

[6] Push-pull influencing; the version included above is based on the model offered by Philip Wickham and Louise Wickham, *Management consulting: delivering an effective project* (3rd edn, 2008, Pearson).

[7] See Stephen Covey's *Seven habits of highly effective people* (2004, Simon and Schuster).

[8] For more information on Nancy Kline's work and approach see *Time to think: listening to ignite the human mind* (2002, Cassell), www.timetothink.com.

[9] Research studies on listening ability (believed and actual) include Howard Beckman's work, as reported by Thomas Maugh III's article, 'Doctor interrupt too quickly, listen too little', in the Los Angeles Times, January 25th, 1999.

[10] Bob Garvey's work on mentoring includes his book *Coaching and mentoring: theory and practice*, co-written with David Megginson and Paul Stokes (2008, Sage).

[11] See the obituary for Marvin Bower in the Daily Telegraph, 30th January 2003.

[12] Kevin Coyne's interview was posted on YouTube on November 16th, 2012. For more information on Kevin Coyne's strategy consulting activities, post McKinsey, see www.thecoynepartnership.com.

[13] Daniel Khaneman, *Thinking, fast and slow* (2012, Penguin).

[14] Dr Steve Peters, *The chimp paradox: the mind management programme to help you achieve success, confidence and happiness* (2012, Vermillion).

[15] Jonanthan Haidt, *The happiness hypothesis: finding modern truth in ancient wisdom* (2006, Basic Books).

[16] For a summary of decision-making biases and heuristics, see Simon Haslam and Ben Shenoy's book, *Strategy decision making: a discovery-led approach* (2017, Kogan Page).

[17] Amos Tversky and Daniel Kahneman talk about anchoring in their 1974 article, 'Judgment under uncertainty: heuristics and biases', *Science*, 185 (4157): 1124–131.

[18] Risk aversion, see Daniel Kahneman and Amos Tversky's 1979 article, 'Prospect theory: an analysis of decision under risk', *Econometrica*, 47 (2): 263.

[19] Phil Rosenzweig talks about hindsight bias in *The halo effect... and the eight other business delusions that deceive managers* (2007, Free Press).

[20] See Margaret Heffernon's book, *Wilful blindness: why we ignore the obvious at our peril'* (2011, Simon & Schuster). Margaret became sensitised to the idea of wilful blindness while reading the trial of the disgraced CEO and Chairman of Enron. In his summing up, Judge Simeon Lake gave his instruction to the jury: 'You may find that a defendant had knowledge of a fact if you find that the defendant deliberately closed his eyes to what would otherwise have been obvious to him. Knowledge can be inferred if the defendant deliberately blinded himself to the existence of a fact'.

[21] Robert Cialdini has international status in the field of influencing and persuasion research, see *Influence: the psychology of persuasion* (rev edn, 2006, Harper Business).

[22] 'Credentialising' describes how consultants both build and communicate their credentials over time. It is a category of the social process of personal legitimising, see Simon Haslam's *Personal legitimising: a substantive grounded theory in the context of small consultancy firms* (1999, PhD thesis, University of Strathclyde).

[23] David Rock's work in the application of neuroscience to leadership and management is bringing a new perspective to understanding human behaviour in the workplace; see, for example, his 2009 article, 'Managing with the brain in mind', *Strategy and Business*, 56.

5
CONCLUSION

Despite similarities between social researchers and consultants as knowledge workers, their work with data, focus on projects and intention to make a positive contribution, there are distinctions between the two ways of working that are potentially fruitful areas of study.

- Social research places emphasis on the understanding, the development of insight or the creation of a conceptual understanding of what is being observed or presented. The focus is the codification or theoretical interpretation – the result of a capably applied programme of systematic investigation –which creates intellectual property and potentially learning to be shared. A consultant is more likely to focus on practice, that is the application of the theory or conceptual understanding – moving the fruits of research on to their application.
- Social research usually places a high emphasis on process and provenance around data (be it qualitative or quantitative) as the foundation of understanding. The higher attention for consultants is typically devoted to 'clients', people affected by the application of research as the recommendation arising from studies are translated into actions. Usually consultants draw heavily on their personal knowledge or experience as it applies to a client situation, which often leads to intellectual property which is unique to a specific context. As such, much of consulting

is to do with change and the implications of things being done differently to the way they have been done to date.

This final chapter summarises the main areas in which consulting practice might add to the repertoire of a social researcher. Below are the key points from the preceding chapters.

Key ingredients of consulting

- Consulting typically involves *independence* of view, *'advising'* (by a range of possible methods) and seeking to be valuable to a client.
- *There can be many stakeholders* that should be considered in a consulting project. Within these are the 'client system', and within the client system is the 'primary client'.
- *Consulting is about change* and effective consulting is mindful of the possible impacts of the consulting intervention on the stakeholders – either during the project or with the implementation of the project's recommendations.
- *A consulting project has a defined scope* – it has a planned beginning and end, agreed deliverables or outputs, and agreed resources devoted to it. The scope of the consulting project seeks to address an issue the client has identified.
- *There are many ways that consultants can bring value to the client* through a consulting project. Consultants can provide the client with skills the client does not have, ideas and insight into sector-leading practice, additional capacity to augment the client's own, objectivity from being detached from the client organisation, and legitimacy through strength of the consultant's brand / credentials. The consultant should be clear as to how the client expects value to be generated.
- *There are three main models of consulting* – 'expert', 'doctor-patient', and 'process'. They all work in different ways and a consultant should be clear about the main model(s) he or she is expected to use during a consulting project.

- *A trust-based relationship with clients is a necessity* – three factors help with the building of trust. These are the consultant's credentials, the consultant's ability to be reliable, and the level of intimacy between consultant and client. A consultant's self-interest (acting in ways that benefit the consultant rather than the client) erodes trust.
- *Consulting, like social research, is not a regulated profession* – this does not mean that consultants cannot behave professionally. Bodies like the International Council for Management Consulting Institutes, for example have developed consulting competence frameworks to encourage good practice in the consulting industry.
- Within professional consulting behaviour sits ethics. Bodies like the International Council for Management Consulting Institutes and the UK's Institute of Consulting provide *ethics guidance for consultants and these should form the platform of Codes of Conduct which consultants can share with their clients.*

The consulting process

- Excellent consulting projects are a result of *consultant and client working together* to the same ends. It is a dual duty. The consultant should work to create the best possible value to the client, and the client should work to make the most of his or her choice of consultant and contribute to the success of the project.
- *Consulting projects typically follow a 'consulting cycle'* which includes agreeing the scope of the work (the contract) near the beginning of the cycle, and the client signing-off on the acceptance of the project deliverables towards the end. The early part of a consulting project typically involves exploring ideas, generating data and building insight. The later phase of the project usually involves focusing on priority areas and shaping recommendations and key actions.
- *A consultant needs to consider assignment intimacy*, which is the degree to which she or he will carry out the consulting work on

the client's site (as distinct from conducting it on the consultant's premises, for example). Providing client and consultant share the understanding of the assignment intimacy, there should be no problems.

- Use of *the pyramid principle can help with the effective design of a consulting project*. In this way the various elements of work in the project can be linked together and sequenced to deliver the top of the pyramid, which is the overall project objective.

- In organisation development and management, practice drives theory and theory guides practice. *Consultants may use management theories or frameworks in consulting projects.* The key skill is to focus on the small number of management ideas that will be the most helpful in a project (less is more).

- Discussions are the stock in trade for many consultants, and *there are guidelines for consultants on how to have productive conversations on consulting projects.* These include being clear on the purpose of the discussion, seeking to build and maintain rapport, and checking facts and details.

- There are *several ways in which consultants can translate data into insight.* The key attributes are curiosity about the data (not taking it at face value) and the 'so-what' question (where the possible implications of the data are played through).

- *The way that recommendations from consulting work are presented to the client needs careful handling.* As well as accomplishing, as a minimum, what the client commissioned, a consultant should be sensitive in the way he/she phrases and sequences recommendations. In this way what needs to be said can be communicated in an effective manner.

Skills in challenging the client

- *Challenging the client's thinking is a positive attribute* in consulting work. Consultants can help clients think in ways they wouldn't otherwise have done.

- The skill for consultants is knowing how, when and on what to *take clients into and out of the ZOUD* (zone of uncomfortable debate) and challenge them appropriately.
- *Different people can view the same thing from different angles –* that is, the same data can conjure up different images in the minds of two people. This is the 'hilltops' metaphor. Much of consulting involves moving beyond the rational view of data and information and focusing on the ways data are interpreted by different people.
- *Frameworks based on psychology and sociology can help consultants to think about how they engage with different people* in order to communicate effectively and appropriately. These frameworks illuminate general guidance which augments the consultant's emotional intelligence qualities.
- In consulting, the concept of *'cognitive distance' relates to the degree to which the consultant is similar to or dissimilar from the client.* Both high and low cognitive distance approaches have their merit in the ways that a consultant can add value to a client, but these ways differ.
- *'Push-pull influencing' is an umbrella term for a range of communication approaches –* 'listening' is widely regarded as the core communication skill in consulting, but a consultant should be proficient in all the communication approaches in push-pull, and have a good feel for when and how to use each.
- *Insight into human decision making has shed light on 'decision bias'.* A consultant should be aware of these biases and how they might colour his or her judgement, and that of the client.
- *The psychology that relates to decision bias can also be applied (assuming ethical practice and positive intent) to influencing clients* to make choices and/or to take action.

The purpose of *Consulting skills for social researchers* has essentially been one of helping insights from one world be offered for transfer to another. Throughout the book we've acknowledged the differences between social research and consulting practice. Hopefully the above provides possible opportunities for social researchers to benefit from some of what the consulting arena has revealed as valuable elements of effective working. The result of social researchers augmenting their technical skills by strengthening their consulting ability can have benefits in several directions. These can range from clearer research project briefs through to greater impact of research findings into policy and practice. Ultimately to the benefit of the societies we serve.

Index

SOCIAL RESEARCH ASSOCIATION SHORTS

Series editors:

Patten Smith, Ipsos MORI Research Methods Centre

Ivana La Valle, University of East London & independent consultant

Social
Research
Association

The SRA Shorts Series is a research methods series in the Policy Press Shorts format. They provide research practitioners, academics and research users with short, high-quality and focused guides to specific topics within the field of social research methods.

The series provides a voice for social research and practical guidance for researchers to improve research quality. It focuses on social research and practice, offering the chance to highlight the impact of research on practice and policy and to draw attention to new and innovative research methods.

Features of the series:

- Books will be between 20 - 50,000 words long, equivalent to 50 - 150 pages.
- The content will be practical and accessible.
- Books will be of interest to an international audience.

Available now:

Demystifying evaluation by David Parsons, Feb 2017